Russian America

ALASKA GEOGRAPHIC® / Volume 26, Number 4 / 1999

To teach many more to better know and more wisely use our natural resources

EDITOR
Penny Rennick

PRODUCTION DIRECTOR
Kathy Doogan

ASSOCIATE EDITOR
Susan Beeman

MARKETING DIRECTOR
Jill S. Brubaker

BOOKKEEPER/DATABASE MANAGER
Claire Whitefield

ADMINISTRATIVE ASSISTANT
Melanie Britton

BOARD OF DIRECTORS
Richard Carlson, Kathy Doogan, Penny Rennick
Robert A. Henning, **PRESIDENT EMERITUS**

ISBN: 1-56661-047-8

PRICE TO NON-MEMBERS THIS ISSUE: $21.95

PRINTED IN U.S.A.

COLOR SEPARATIONS: Graphic Chromatics
PRINTING: Banta Publications Group / Hart Press

POSTMASTER:
Send address changes to:
ALASKA GEOGRAPHIC®
P.O. Box 93370, Anchorage, Alaska 99509-3370

COVER: *Anchorage artist Byron Birdsall painted this icon titled "The Four Saints of Alaska"(© Byron Birdsall 1987)*

PREVIOUS PAGE: *Shelikof Strait between Kodiak and the Alaska mainland is named for Grigorii Shelikhov, prime mover behind the Russian American Co. (Fred Hirschmann)*

FACING PAGE: *This altar in the Russian Bishop's House in Sitka has been restored to its 1850's appearance. (Fred Hirschmann)*

ALASKA GEOGRAPHIC® (ISSN 0361-1353) is published quarterly by The Alaska Geographic Society, 639 West International Airport Rd., Unit 38, Anchorage, AK 99518. Periodicals postage paid at Anchorage, Alaska, and additional mailing offices. Copyright © 1999 The Alaska Geographic Society. All rights reserved. Registered trademark: Alaska Geographic, ISSN 0361-1353; key title Alaska Geographic. This issue published Nov. 1999.

THE ALASKA GEOGRAPHIC SOCIETY is a non-profit, educational organization dedicated to improving geographic understanding of Alaska and the North, putting geography back in the classroom and exploring new methods of teaching and learning.

MEMBERS RECEIVE *ALASKA GEOGRAPHIC®*, a high-quality, colorful quarterly that devotes each issue to monographic, in-depth coverage of a specific northern region or resource-oriented subject. Back issues are also available (see p. 96). Membership is $49 ($59 to non-U.S. addresses) per year. To order or to request a free catalog of back issues, contact: Alaska Geographic Society, P.O. Box 93370, Anchorage, AK 99509-3370; phone (907) 562-0164 or toll free (888) 255-6697, fax (907) 562-0479, e-mail: akgeo@akgeo.com, web: www.akgeo.com

SUBMITTING PHOTOGRAPHS: Those interested in submitting photos for possible publication should write for a list of upcoming topics or other photo needs and a copy of our editorial guidelines. We cannot be responsible for unsolicited submissions. Any submission not accompanied by sufficient postage for return by certified mail will be returned by regular mail.

CHANGE OF ADDRESS: When you move, the post office will not automatically forward your *ALASKA GEOGRAPHIC®*. To ensure continuous service, please notify us at least six weeks before moving. Send your new address and membership number or a mailing label from a recent issue of *ALASKA GEOGRAPHIC®* to: Alaska Geographic Society, Box 93370, Anchorage, AK 99509-3370.

If your book is returned to us by the post office because it is undeliverable, we will contact you to ask if you wish to receive a replacement for a small fee to cover additional postage.

The Library of Congress has cataloged this serial publication as follows:

Alaska Geographic. v.1-
    [Anchorage, Alaska Geographic Society] 1972-
    v. ill. (part col.). 23 x 31 cm.
    Quarterly
    Official publication of The Alaska Geographic Society.
    Key title: Alaska geographic, ISSN 0361-1353.

    1. Alaska—Description and travel—1959-
    —Periodicals. I. Alaska Geographic Society.

F901.A266 917.98'04'505 72-92087

Library of Congress 75[79112] MARC-S.

ABOUT THIS ISSUE:
    Written by some of the field's noted scholars, *Russian America* offers a snapshot of Alaska's richly textured decades under Russian rule. We are indebted to many researchers who contributed to this volume including state historian Jo Antonson; archaeologist Erik Hilsinger, both of the state Office of History and Archaeology; archivists Diane Brenner and Mina Jacobs at the Anchorage Museum of History and Art; librarian and Alaska bibliographer Bruce Merrell, Anchorage Municipal Libraries; collections curator Steve Henrikson, Alaska State Museum; Kay Shelton, head of historical collections, Alaska State Library; and Sylvie Savage, archives library technician, University of Alaska Fairbanks.

    Name spellings conform to Richard A. Pierce's *Russian America: A Biographical Dictionary* (1990), an invaluable resource for scholars and lay readers alike.

    More than 200 years after explorers sailed east for Alaska shores, the state's Russian past remains the subject of intense secular and church scholarship on both sides of Bering Strait. Attention is warranted: While Russian authorities ably documented certain aspects of colony life, other realms such as Alaska Native roles are still being explored.

    We welcome these advances and apologize to any readers who may wonder why a particular nuance has not found its way to our pages. Researching *Russian America* was a lot like being given a set of matrushka dolls, the Russian toy in which larger dolls are taken apart to reveal ever-smaller dolls nested inside. One piece of history led us, tantalizingly, to another and another until like the smallest matrushka, our space simply was gone. ∎

 # Contents

Russian America:
A Place to Start

By Lydia Black

Before Alaska came under the sovereignty of the United States on Oct. 18, 1867, this vast land of rich resources and diverse people was part of the Russian Empire. Russian rule was relatively short-lived, about 135 years, but Russian influence was profound and in many sections of Alaska it is felt to this day.

For indigenous people such as the Aleut, Alutiiq, Chugach, Dena'ina Athabaskan, Tlingit and Haida who came in direct contact with Russian hunters, traders and explorers, the period was one of rapid change. While early explorers and settlements generally were spread along southern coastal Alaska, Russia's presence was felt as far inland as the Interior, home of the Athabaskan, and as far west as the Bering Sea region, where the Yupik and Inupiat live. Contact with indigenous peoples stemmed primarily from fur trading, the economic exchange that linked Native Alaskans to the worldwide net of commerce.

But Russia's influence went far beyond geographic boundaries: Missionaries introduced teachings of the Russian Orthodox Church and crafted some of the earliest alphabets of Native languages. Schools were opened where instruction was bilingual, and often trilingual. Pioneering efforts at public health were introduced when hospitals were established in outposts and smallpox vaccinations were made available. Horticulture, livestock-keeping, new tools and skills, and the use of firearms spread through the colony. Initial efforts to limit marine mammal harvests to sustainable levels also occurred during this time.

Change did not come at the same time or even with the same impact in all parts of sparsely settled Alaska. It is worth noting that, unlike the pioneer eras of other western states, Alaska under imperial rule did not see a large influx of settlers eager to

FACING PAGE: *A National Historic Landmark, the Russian Orthodox Church of the Holy Ascension of Christ welcomes the faithful at Unalaska. Parts of the church date to 1825, when Unalaska was a center for Russian Orthodoxy in Alaska. (Dan Parrett)*

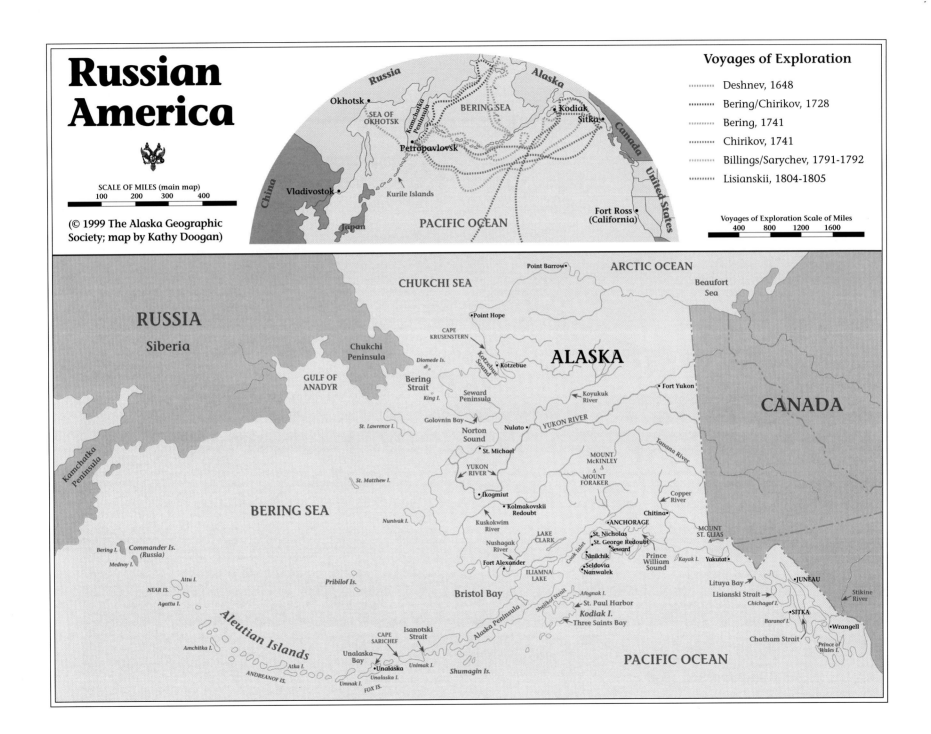

Russian America

SCALE OF MILES (main map)
100   200   300   400

(© 1999 The Alaska Geographic Society; map by Kathy Doogan)

Voyages of Exploration

.... Deshnev, 1648
.... Bering/Chirikov, 1728
.... Bering, 1741
.... Chirikov, 1741
.... Billings/Sarychev, 1791-1792
.... Lisianskii, 1804-1805

Voyages of Exploration Scale of Miles
400   800   1200   1600

Russia
Okhotsk
SEA OF OKHOTSK
Kamchatka Peninsula
Petropavlovsk
Vladivostok
China
Japan
Kurile Islands
BERING SEA
Alaska
Kodiak
Sitka
Canada
United States
Fort Ross (California)
PACIFIC OCEAN

Point Barrow
CHUKCHI SEA
ARCTIC OCEAN
Beaufort Sea
RUSSIA
Siberia
Point Hope
CAPE KRUSENSTERN
Diomede Is.
Kotzebue
Kotzebue Sound
ALASKA
Chukchi Peninsula
GULF OF ANADYR
Bering Strait
King I.
Seward Peninsula
Koyukuk River
Fort Yukon
CANADA
Golovnin Bay
St. Lawrence I.
Nulato
YUKON RIVER
Norton Sound
St. Michael
Tanana River
MOUNT McKINLEY
MOUNT FORAKER
St. Matthew I.
YUKON RIVER
Kamchatka Peninsula
Ikogmiut
Copper River
Kolmakovskii Redoubt
Chitina
BERING SEA
Nunivak I.
Kuskokwim River
ANCHORAGE
MOUNT ST. ELIAS
LAKE CLARK
St. Nicholas
St. George Redoubt
Seward
Bering I.
Commander Is. (Russia)
Nushagak River
Ninilchik
Prince William Sound
Kayak I.
Yakutat
Mednoy I.
Fort Alexander
Seldovia
Nanwalek
Cook Inlet
ILIAMNA LAKE
Attu I.
NEAR IS.
Pribilof Is.
Bristol Bay
Afognak I.
Shelikof Strait
Lituya Bay
JUNEAU
Agattu I.
St. Paul Harbor
Kodiak I.
Three Saints Bay
Lisianski Strait
Chichagof I.
Stikine River
Aleutian Islands
CAPE SARICHEF
Isanotski Strait
Alaska Peninsula
Baranof I.
SITKA
Amchitka I.
Atka I.
Unalaska Bay
Unimak I.
Shumagin Is.
Wrangell
Chatham Strait
ANDREANOF IS.
Unalaska
Unalaska I.
PACIFIC OCEAN
Prince of Wales I.
Umnak I.
FOX IS.

This statue honors Aleksandr Baranov, who retired at age 71 after 27 years as chief manager of the Russian American Co. at Kodiak and later Sitka. The company saw its most prosperous years under the experienced trader, who was an aggressive administrator. During his tenure Novoarkhangelsk (Sitka) was founded, and secular schools for Russian and Aleut children were established. (Ernest Manewal)

clear 40-acre homesteads in the wilderness. Russians in Alaska never numbered more than 800; most often, they numbered 400 or fewer, most living in Novoarkhangelsk (New Archangel), the capital of Russian America at present-day Sitka. Russians were dispersed at small outposts, the largest at Kodiak and Unalaska.

In fact, the Russian government forbade permanent settlement of Alaska by Russian citizens arriving from the mother country. No one was authorized to claim Native land or take up residence in a Native community. Most Russian citizens stayed only for the duration of their labor contract; after 1799, contracts were with the monopoly Russian American Co., chartered that year.

A few Russians married in the colony and established families but husbands and fathers who wished to remain in Alaska had to petition the government for permission. Known as Creoles, the sons and daughters of these Russian men were at home in Native communities, speaking both their own languages and Russian. Creoles were a bridge between two cultures and became agents of change. Through education, a Native middle class emerged, bound by kinship and sentiment both to Alaska and Russia. These men and women were the mainstay of Russian America.

From inception, the Russian American Co. was among Europe's major fur trading ventures. But by

This engraving from a painting by Luka Voronin, expedition artist with the Billings/Sarychev voyage of 1790-92, shows the early days of Russian settlement at Three Saints Bay. (From Sarychev's Atlas; courtesy of Alaska and Polar Regions Archives, Rasmuson Library, University of Alaska Fairbanks, C0015, Page 28)

the mid-19th century, fur markets began to shrink, prompting the company to consider diversification, a move that was interrupted by world events. Europe, China and the Far East all were adapting to the aftermath of the Opium War of 1839 to 1842, when China ceded Hong Kong to England; and the Crimean War of 1853 to 1856, in which Russia was defeated by England and its allies. Fearing England's expansion to Alaska from its foothold in British Columbia, Russia invited a friendly power — the United States — to buy the colony. Alaska was "sold."

The rights of Russian citizens and several Native groups were to be protected by terms of the U.S.-Russia treaty. In fact, neither the military government nor the early civil government cared much for the treaty's terms: Alaska was to be Americanized, and the role of the Orthodox Church, a dominant element of many communities, was minimized. Popular histories marked the beginning of "real" Alaska with the Klondike gold strikes of the 1890s, which were centered in the Yukon but drew thousands to neighboring Alaska.

Misconception persists today. Americans who may know that Alaska once was part of Russia often can recite only a catalog of stereotypes: They think Russians came in greed and in search of riches, to enslave Natives and despoil the land of furbearers, only to sell out for a few million dollars.

So much of Russian American heritage is lost through these representations. But scholars, many of them working in Alaska, now recognize the complexities of Russia's presence in North America. New materials on a wide range of issues are being published so that today a curious reader is rewarded with information about early explorations, free-booters and the all-pervasive Russian American Co. On the eve of a new century, we Alaskans join the rest of the world in considering the past to understand our future; for us, Russian America is a place to start.

America Lies To The East

Beginning with the 15th century, Russian pioneers dwelling in the northern provinces and White Sea coastal region were moving east. By the middle of the 16th century, the kingdom of Sibir' on the great rivers Ob' and Irtysh was conquered and offered as a gift to the ruler of Muscovite State. Less than 100 years later, early explorers known as *pervoprokhodsty* (pathfinders) reached the shores of the Arctic Ocean from the White Sea to the Chukchi Peninsula. From the peninsula, a region known as Chukotka, they were able to stand on Pacific and Arctic ocean shores.

In the north, the advance moved from one great river basin to another. Early explorers traveled by sea, from river mouth to river mouth, ascending mighty Siberian waterways. Upstream in inland Siberia, portages were made river to river, ultimately descending to the Arctic Ocean. Outposts were built on the Kolyma River and on the Kamchatka Peninsula. Adventurers by 1648 had sailed through present-day Bering Strait from north to south; soon after, an outpost was established on the Anadyr River emptying into the Bering Sea.

In Chukotka and northern Kamchatka, these Russian pioneers heard tales about a great land beyond the sea. They even encountered prisoners of the Chukchi and Koryak peoples who were captured in raids in the far off land. When rumors and the reports of local officials reached the Russian capital, experts there determined this "Great Land" was America. The realization prompted Peter the Great to plan official exploration of the foreign coast; on his deathbed, he signed orders dispatching a Russian navy vessel to the northern ocean and on to America.

In 1728, Vitus Bering in the St. Gabriel passed through the strait which today bears his name. Bering named St. Lawrence Island on this voyage but the coast of the American continent was not explored. Under one of Peter's successors, Empress Anna, the government organized a large-scale effort to investigate and chart the entire coast of the Arctic Ocean, the Okhotsk and Bering seas and to explore the northwest coast of North America. This effort, begun in the 1730s, is known as the Second Kamchatka Expedition.

As part of this expedition, the St. Gabriel, with a detachment led by Afanasii Shestakov, was once again dispatched from Okhotsk and Kamchatka. In 1732, the vessel visited the Diomedes and made landfall at Cape Prince of Wales on Alaska's Seward

Volcanoes are one hallmark of Russia's Kamchatka Peninsula, which lies west of the Aleutian and Commander islands and was the launching point for many early Russian expeditions. Explorer Vitus Bering suspected a "Great Land" lay to the east as certain birds migrated regularly, and pine and other uprooted trees not found growing in Kamchatka sometimes washed ashore there. (From Sarychev's Atlas; *courtesy of the Anchorage Museum of History and Art)*

Fort Ross

By Mike Doogan

EDITOR'S NOTE: *On glimpsing the verdant northern California landscape in 1824, explorer Otto von Kotzebue, whose travels had taken him from Bering Strait to the South Pacific, had a single thought: corn.*

"I could not help but speculate," wrote von Kotzebue, envisioning "an inexhaustible granary" capable of sustaining the isolated outposts of Kamchatka, Okhotsk and Russian America. "(These) regions so often afflicted with a scarcity of corn, would derive new life from a close connection with California."

It was a reasonable but unrealized dream; 25 years after the Russian American Co. became a chartered monopoly in Alaska, the colony remained dependent on a supply line that stretched 8,000 miles from central Asia to Sitka, a route that relied on barges, horses and ships and too often left the colonists foraging for themselves. In addition to farmland, Russian authorities looked south for fresh populations of sea otters after Alaska populations dwindled from decades of overhunting.

With construction of Fort Ross in 1812, Russians became the first Europeans to settle in California north of San Francisco.

The winter of 1805-06 was particularly bad and food was so scarce in Sitka that a visiting Russian American Co. official, Nikolai Rezanov, sailed to California in an attempt to get supplies. At the Presidio of San Francisco, Rezanov encountered the official rejection and unofficial acceptance that was to characterize Russian-Spanish relations in California.

Officially, all California ports were closed to foreigners and trade with them was forbidden; but Spain was far away and the mission fathers were eager to trade their crops for manufactured goods. Rezanov swapped English cloth, linen, leather boots, saws and axes for barley, peas and beans. He also noted that the coast north of San Francisco was wide open.

Knowing there were both furs and food available, Aleksandr Baranov sent his chief assistant, Ivan Kuskov, on a series of exploratory trips. In 1811, Kuskov selected a site about 75 miles north of San Francisco for a permanent base of operations. The following year, he returned with 25 Russians and 80 Alaska Natives and erected Fort Ross. A rebuilt version of the Kuskov house, named in the manager's honor, stands at the fort today.

From the outside, Fort Ross looks much the same as it did nearly 190 years ago: The structure sits on a slightly sloping bluff, about 100 feet above two coves that today belong mainly to seals. Its walls are 12 feet high, built of squared-off logs with pointed tops planted into the ground — a palisade, in military jargon.

Blockhouses jut out from the northeast and southwest corners, built to allow defenders to fire along all four walls without shooting into one another. At first the fort boasted 12 cannons, a number that grew in time to 40. Cannons in the southwest

blockhouse have a clear field of fire to the sea. The Russians called the place Colony Ross or Ross Office, but the Spanish called it what it was — a fort.

While Ross-based hunters found early success in targeting sea otter for the fur trade, the animals were quickly depleted. In his report on Russian America, company official Kirill Khlebnikov noted that otter taken along the coast from Point Arena to Drake's Bay, a distance of about 80 miles, declined from 114 prime animals and 39 yearlings in 1815, to just 39 prime otters and four yearlings taken in 1822 and 1823 combined.

Farming did not prosper either. The amount of land available at the fort was

Not all exploration was done on a grand scale in Russian America. The naturalist's eye for detail and note-taking contributed to mapping lands in the colony. (Steve Henrikson)

Russian explorers and traders had grand plans of feeding the whole of Russian America with crops grown on lands in western North America north of Spanish-held territory. But Fort Ross, the first Russian settlement in California north of San Francisco, was an agricultural bust and became a trading center for other goods. (Harry M. Walker)

limited. Frequent coastal fog brought wheat rust. Gophers, squirrels and mice ate the crops. And the Russians, Alaska Natives and local Indians, called the Kashaya Pomo, were neither enthusiastic nor scientific farmers. Different locations were tried farther inland but the crop production never met the goal of feeding the rest of Russian America.

The Russians did produce a variety of goods at the fort — plows, axes, nails, pots and pans, and blankets — so the post became a center of trade with the Californians, including the mission fathers who exchanged goods for food that either was eaten at Fort Ross or sent north.

A number of factors kept the Russians from trying to settle more of California: Russia was a long way away and had become increasingly interested in developing Asia. Mexico encouraged settlement of northern California, granting all the land around the Russian holdings to its own citizens. In 1823, the Monroe Doctrine stated that American lands no longer were open for colonizing by Europeans; in 1824, Russia signed a treaty with the United States promising not to settle south of the famous 54-40 line.

In 1841, the Russians sold out: After failing to interest the Hudson's Bay Co., the French and the Mexicans, Fort Ross's moveable inventory, but not the land, was sold to German immigrant John Sutter for $30,000. (A bankrupt Sutter eventually left California for Pennsylvania after gold hunters in 1848 swarmed his mill near Sacramento.)

While never living up to von Kotzebue's dream, Fort Ross was a tribute to Russian industriousness. Starting with nothing in 1812, the official inventory at the time of sale to Sutter included "a square fort of logs 1,088 feet in circumference, 12 feet high with two watchtowers," as well as several houses, barracks, three warehouses, a kitchen, jail, and chapel with belfry and dome. Outside the fort were baths, 10 kitchens and 24 houses, most with an orchard; there was a tannery, blacksmith, bakery, dairy house and boathouse as well as two windmills for grinding, three threshing floors and a hog pen.

Today, after enduring a fire in 1970 and the rerouting in 1972 of Highway 1 that ran through the site, Fort Ross State Historic Park sees more than 250,00 visitors a year. Restorations, including rebuilding a chapel knocked down in the 1906 earthquake, have added replica muskets, cannons and period tools. Living History Day, held each July, involves some 100 costumed volunteers and staff staging history re-enactments, cannon firings and occasional Russian dancing. Says state park ranger Dan Murley, "It's quite a day." ▫

Mike Doogan is an Anchorage Daily News columnist. This piece is excerpted with permission from "A Russian Outpost," Aug. 11, 1991, Anchorage Daily News.

Peninsula. In 1741, a two-vessel navy contingent under the overall command of Bering sailed for Alaska's Pacific coast. A vessel under Aleksei Chirikov, Bering's second in command, made landfall in Tlingit territory in Southeast Alaska. Bering's ship took on water at Kayak Island and entered Prince William Sound before sailing west toward the Shumagin Islands near the southern tip of the Alaska Peninsula. In treaties adopted in 1824 and 1825 with the United States and Great Britain respectively, these landfalls would serve to draw Alaska's boundaries.

On the return voyage to Kamchatka, Bering's ship was wrecked in 1741 on one of the uninhabited Commander Islands, known today as Bering Island. Bering died there and his island gravesite is venerated today. Crewmen who made it through the winter built a small vessel from salvaged materials and sailed for Kamchatka while Chirikov ventured east once again, searching for Bering. (Chirikov came close to Amchitka in the Aleutian Islands.)

Fresh Prospects

One can only imagine how word of the Great Land spread through Russian settlements, where most earned a living hunting seals, walrus, fur seals

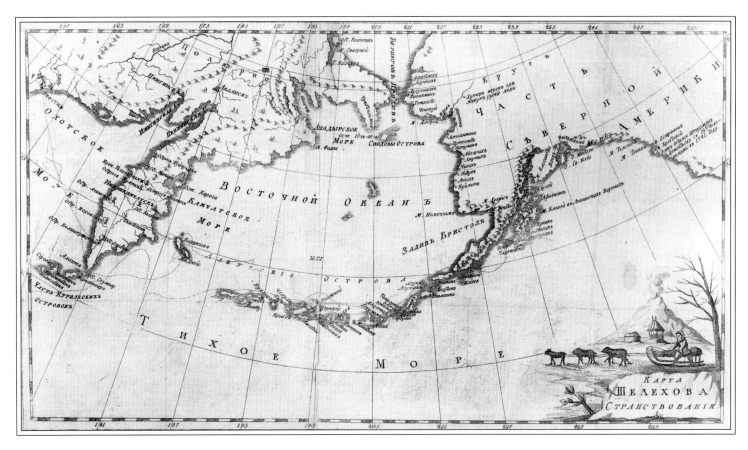

FACING PAGE: *This map shows Grigorii Shelikhov's voyages in the North Pacific and Bering Sea. Originally from Ryl'sk, a small trading center, where his family were merchants, Shelikhov traveled north to Iakutsk and then to Okhotsk where he gained experience in trading in 1774. He decried the wastefulness of the intense competition among the fur traders and proposed a monopoly be given for trade on the North American mainland and in the Aleutian and Kurile islands. (Alaska and Polar Regions Archives, Rasmuson Library, University of Alaska Fairbanks, Plate 182, 1793 Rare Map Col.)*

ABOVE: *Trading ships from various nations, marine mammal hunters and fishermen support the thriving commerce enjoyed by Sitka in the early 1800s. To protect this trade, Aleksandr Baranov had built a sturdy fort on Castle Hill overlooking the harbor. (Illustration from the 1803-1806 round-the-world voyage of Capt. Ivan Kruzenshtern and naval officer Iurii Lisianskii)*

and sea otters. News that the waters off north-western North America were rich in these furbearers offered fresh prospects for pioneering entrepreneurs bold enough to sail these waters. Once again, these early adventurers outpaced government efforts to open new lands and in 1743 vessels landed on Bering Island. In 1745 Russians were on Copper Island, also known as Mednoy Island, the second of the Commander Islands. One ship wintered at Attu.

Here the fur hunter-entrepreneurs known as *promyshlenniki* encountered the Aleuts, as the Attuans called themselves. The Russians were not welcome: Aleuts resisted foreign intrusion and brutal conflict ensued. Some Russians later were tried and punished but despite government efforts to curb violence, the pattern was repeated in islands to the east where "Americans," as the Russians called

inhabitants of the Aleutians east of the Near Islands, were more numerous and organized warfare was practiced by the Natives.

By 1764, Russian ships reached Kodiak Island, roughly 1,500 miles east of Attu. By 1778, Unalaska Bay was a permanent harbor for Russian vessels that sailed into Cook Inlet and Prince William Sound throughout the 1780s. In 1784, Irkutsk merchant Grigorii Shelikhov conquered Kodiak Islanders by force — in violation of Russian law — in an attack known today as the Refuge Rock massacre. As early as 1786, work crews were taken to the uninhabited Pribilof Islands to harvest fur seals.

While Catherine the Great supported Russia's fur entrepreneurs, the government also wanted to establish Russian rule in territory the empire now claimed for its own. Naval expeditions were twice dispatched to Alaska. In 1768, a two-vessel squadron under captains Petr Krenitsyn and Mikhail Levashov was sent to the Aleutians with a secret assignment. The ships were to intercept another navy squadron, under the command of Adm. Vasilii Chichagov, that had been dispatched from the Kola Peninsula in northwestern Russia

ABOVE LEFT: *Russian explorers admired and took advantage of the Aleuts' hunting and survival skills such as use of the* atlatl, *or throwing stick, and the art of making baidarkas or kayaks. (From Sarychev's* Atlas; *courtesy of Alaska and Polar Regions Archives, Rasmuson Library, University of Alaska Fairbanks, C0015, Plate 162)*

LEFT: *By the 1860s, just before the United States bought Alaska, Novoarchangelsk had grown considerably. The Governor's House at right and St. Michael's Cathedral, with its 84-foot-tall bell tower, are easily identified in this painting by an unknown artist, said to be assigned to the Russian navy. (File photo)*

SITKA.
VIEW OF THE TOWN FROM THE SOUTH-WEST, MOUNT EDGECOMB BEARING EAST.

RIGHT: *The Rev. Ioann Veniaminov on first sailing to Russian America is depicted in this painting by Nikolai Solomin, currently one of Russia's top artists. Solomin, recently retired from the Russian army, served in Afghanistan as combat artist. One of his paintings was presented as a gift of state to President Bill Clinton from Russian President Boris Yeltsin. Solomin was close to his grandmother who ensured that the youngster maintained ties with Russian Orthodoxy. Currently Solomin is in charge of restoring Spasky Cathedral in Moscow. (Ernest Manewal)*

BELOW RIGHT: *Nearly 215 years after he first sighted North America, Vitus Bering's image and name remained a viable marketing force. This box of fine cigars passed U.S. Customs in 1953. (Courtesy of Douglas Veltre)*

and to explore the shortest route from northern Russia to America across the pole.

The vessels wintered at Isanotski Strait and in Captain's Bay on Unalaska but Chichagov, stopped by ice, failed to arrive. This expedition provided the Russian government with the first survey maps of the eastern Aleutians based on astronomical observations while Levashov's ethnographic notes and sketches to this day serve as primary data on eastern Aleut culture.

Disturbed by the ever-increasing presence of British ships in Alaska waters following the voyage of Capt. James Cook in 1778, Russia mustered a powerful naval force to claim territory from California to Bering Strait and points east in 1786. The main squadron was to sail around the world by departing from Kronstadt, Russia's naval base on the Baltic Sea, but was pressed into service elsewhere when wars broke out with Sweden and Turkey.

A second group of vessels was made ready at Okhotsk under the command of explorer Joseph Billings, a British officer in Russian service; Roman

"traffic where they please, I will supply neither men, nor money, nor ships." Following her death in 1796, that policy changed when her son and heir, Emperor Paul I, granted a monopoly to exploit Alaska's resources to a company managed by Shelikhov's heirs in 1799. (Shelikhov died in 1795.)

With establishment of the government-chartered Russian American Co., Shelikhov's competitors had to withdraw and company headquarters at Kodiak became a springboard for expansion to the mainland. The western and central Aleutians reverted almost totally to a local subsistence economy while the eastern Aleutians, Pribilofs, Kodiak archipelago and Pacific coastal communities of the Alaska Peninsula became a kingdom ruled by company manager Aleksandr Baranov. The people of this broad region became a source of company labor; armed resistance against the intruder was impossible. These conditions persisted for nearly 20 years when the Russian government began curtailing exploitation of Native peoples.

Gall (also known as Robert Hall), of English origin who joined the Russian navy when he was 15; and Gavriil Sarychev, a Russian naval officer. This squadron sailed from 1790 to 1792, compiling rich data that has yet to be studied in full although Sarychev's account was published in 1802. In 1811, Sarychev published excerpts of data gathered by Gall.

Neither Men, Nor Money, Nor Ships

There is little doubt that the history of Alaska's Russian period would be different had Catherine II lived longer. An advocate of laissez-faire economics, she once declared that while traders were free to

Times changed for Russians too; the "old voyagers," the men who had opened Alaska for Russia, saw the end of freebooting days and served the Russian American Co. as hired labor. A few became enthusiastic supporters of Baranov, sailing for him to the Columbia River, which today forms the Washington-Oregon boundary, and as far south as California and Hawaii. Others, mostly aged men, returned to Russia to die in their homeland; still others stayed put, married Native women and raised Alaska families. A few of these Russian names survive today among Native descendants, but many are lost in anonymous graves. ▪

Now retired and living in Kodiak where she is organizing the archives of the Russian Orthodox seminary, Dr. Lydia Black is a former professor of anthropology at the University of Alaska in Fairbanks.

A Chronology of Russian America

By Rosanne Pagano
and Joan Antonson

1648: Seafarer Semen Dezhnev sails through straits separating Asia and North America; Siberian Natives tell him of a large, mountainous land to the east.

1689-1725: Peter I (the Great) initiates the Westernization of Russia, adopting administrative reforms but also expanding autocracy and serfdom. He pursues expansion for commercial purposes and in 1703 establishes the new capital at St. Petersburg.

July 21, 1728: Vitus Bering, a Danish seaman in Russian service, and naval officer Aleksei Chirikov, Bering's second in command, sail north from the Kamchatka Peninsula in the packet boat St. Gabriel, navigating the strait eventually named for Bering. The explorers sight and name St. Lawrence Island and the Diomede Islands.

Although the St. Gabriel does not sight

This Russian postage stamp celebrates the 250th anniversary of Vitus Bering's sighting and naming of Mount St. Elias in 1741. (Ernest Manewal)

mainland Alaska, Bering concludes that the New World and Asia are separate land masses based on talks with Natives who approached his boat.

1732: Explorers Ivan Fedorov and Mikhail Gvozdev reach King Island and get information from a Native about the Alaska coast.

June 1741: Bering leads a second North Pacific expedition with Chirikov, departing in two small wooden ships, the St. Peter and the St. Paul, from the Kamchatka Peninsula port of Petropavlovsk. Aboard the St. Peter is noted German naturalist Georg Steller, first to record coastal Alaska wildlife.

July 1741: Chirikov, captain of the St. Paul, sights the forested Alexander Archipelago in Southeast Alaska. Two small boats are dispatched for shore but fail to return, prompting Chirikov to conclude that Americans seen paddling near his ship had killed or detained the men. Dismayed, Chirikov begins the return voyage to Kamchatka, arriving Oct. 8.

July 1741: Five days after Chirikov, Bering reports his first sighting of the Alaska mainland. Bering, aboard the St. Peter, names a snow-capped volcano on the southcentral coast St. Elias.

Steller, who accompanies crewmen going ashore for water, collects artifacts that prompt him to conclude Alaska's indigen-

ous people share attributes with Siberian Natives.

Sailing west for home, Bering stops at the Shumagin Islands off the Alaska Peninsula's southern coast and names them in memory of a crewman buried there.

Dec. 8, 1741: Bering dies of scurvy after being shipwrecked on an island ultimately named for him; hunting sustains survivors through the winter. Crewmen build a small boat from wreckage of the St. Peter, reaching Kamchatka on Aug. 26, 1742.

Bering's men are laden with pelts — seal, fox and the highly prized sea otter — and the news stirs frontiersmen eager to exploit New World riches. Discoveries by Bering and Chirikov, such as the approximate location of the Aleutian Islands, guide fur traders. By the late 18th century, Russian seafarers have made landfalls and established trading posts in the Aleutian Islands, Kodiak Island, the Alaska Peninsula, Cook Inlet, Prince William Sound and Southeast Alaska.

1742: On a second voyage in the St. Paul, Chirikov sights Attu Island but is turned back by foul weather.

1743: Emel'ian Basov, a Kamchatka-based sergeant, sails for Bering Island with two veterans of the Bering expedition in search of furs. Basov is among the first Russian fur hunter-entrepreneurs known as *promyshlenniki.*

1745: Russian fur hunters establish a camp on Attu after skirmishing with Natives there and at Agattu Island.

1749: Russian hunters try to extract tribute payment, known as *iasak,* in the form of furs from Aleutian Island Natives.

1752: The vessel St. Ioann returns to Petropavlovsk from an Aleutian expedition, hauling sea otter and blue fox pelts — 700 each. Chinese merchants pay premium prices and Alaska's fur boom begins in earnest.

1759: Fur trader and explorer Ivan Stepanovich Glotov reaches Umnak Island, roughly 300 miles west of the Alaska Peninsula, and spends three winters hunting sea otter and fox. The group of eastern Aleutian Islands is named Fox Islands.

1761: Gavriil Pushkarev goes ashore on the Alaska Peninsula. Andreian Tolstykh discovers the middle group of Aleutian islands, named Andreanof in his honor.

1762: Catherine II becomes empress of Russia undertaking wars and expanding Russia's borders. She reigns to 1796.

1763: Aleuts attack four Russian vessels at Unalaska, Unimak and Umnak islands. At least 80 Russians are killed; they brutally retaliate, killing more than 200 Aleuts.

September 1763: Glotov discovers Kodiak Island and unsuccessfully demands tribute from Natives who mount an attack. Glotov winters at Kodiak and discovers neighboring Afognak Island.

1764: Fur trader Ivan Solov'ev reaches Unalaska and remains for the winter. Atrocities against Aleuts allegedly committed by Solov'ev are reported to the Russian government.

March 2, 1766: Catherine II formally acknowledges the discovery and accession of six Aleutian islands, admonishing fur

The Russian Bishop's House, originally hewn from Sitka spruce, is now rebuilt and restored to its period condition. Its colonial architecture and lush furnishings housed Bishop Innocent (Ioann Veniaminov) and his staff. (Ernest Manewal)

hunters to treat Native residents ("your new brothers") with "gentleness, neither oppressing nor cheating them."

The decree is largely ignored; *promyshlenniki* adopt a lawless credo, "God is in His heaven and the czar is far away," and force Aleuts to hunt for them, sometimes taking hostages to compel compliance.

1766-69: A secret government expedition led by Mikhail Levashov and Petr Krenitsyn explores the Aleutian Islands. A map based on this sailing is heavily relied on by subsequent voyagers. Russia enjoys a monopoly in North Pacific fur exports to Asia.

1768: The Steller sea cow, relative of the manatee, is hunted to extinction by *promyshlenniki* seeking food.

1770: The Lebedev-Lastochkin Co. builds a warehouse and supply station at Unalaska that is occupied intermittently.

1772: After sailing the length of the Aleutians to the Alaska Peninsula, explorer Potap Zaikov spends three years gathering observations. He produces an accurate map and his log is published by the Russian Academy of Sciences.

1774: Spain's Juan Perez sails the Santiago north from Mexico and sights the southern tip of present-day Prince of Wales Island, in Southeast Alaska. Noting an old bayonet and iron pieces in the possession of Natives, Perez concludes the relics are from Chirikov's expedition of 1741. The finding becomes a key to establishing the southern boundary of Russian claims in North America at 54 degrees 40'N.

May 1778: British Capt. James Cook sails through Southeast Alaska waters and into Southcentral, exploring the Anchorage-area inlet that today bears his name; he voyages on through the Bering Sea and Bering Strait. Cook prepares the first reliable maps of the Pacific Northwest coast and notes ethnographic similarities between Alaska Natives and indigenous peoples of Greenland.

While acknowledging the region's potential fur wealth, Cook concludes it is of limited value to Britain unless a northern sea route is found. Cook's men, making a return trip by the China Sea, realize breathtaking prices for sea otter furs in Canton.

1778: An estimated 500 Russians hunt and trade for furs at Fox Island settlements at Umnak, Unalaska and neighboring sites.

1780: Fur hunting companies move into Cook Inlet waters. Five large operations are in place by 1780. In 1781, a fur trading company owned by Grigorii Shelikhov and

Medals were prized by Russian explorers. These belonged to Prince Dmitrii Maksutov, last governor of Russian America, from 1865-67. (#III-R-380/81, Alaska State Museum)

Ivan Golikov enters the trade; in 20 years its syndicate of merchant-traders would become the Russian American Co.

1784: Shelikhov and his wife, Natal'ia, establish a post at Kodiak's Three Saints Bay, considered to be the first continuously inhabited Russian settlement in Alaska. Alutiiq Natives trying to evade the intruders gather at Refuge Rock on Sitkalidak Island but are ambushed by cannon fire; many jump to their deaths. The massacre is part of the Russian subjugation of Kodiak Island Natives.

1786: Working for Lebedev-Lastochkin and Shelikhov, navigator Gavriil Pribylov discovers the Pribilof Islands. He names the two main islands St. Paul and St. George. The islands are breeding grounds for millions of northern fur seals. Aleuts are relocated to the Pribilofs to hunt.

1787: St. George Redoubt, the first perm- anent Russian settlement on mainland Alaska, is established as a ship-building site at the mouth of the Kasilof River on the Kenai Peninsula.

1787-92: Joseph Billings, a British seaman in Russian service, and naval officer Gavriil Sarychev work to map the North Pacific. Cape Sarichef in the Aleutian Islands and Sarichef Strait in the Bering Sea are named for Sarychev.

1790: Shelikhov hires Aleksandr Baranov to

manage Southcentral Alaska operations. Baranov drives out regional competition.

In 1799, Baranov becomes the first Russian American Co. chief manager and expands Russian fur hunting into Southeast Alaska. Politically astute and renowned for parties, Baranov would foil a murder plot in 1809, guide the Russian American Co. to its best financial years of 1813-14, and marry a Native woman and raise two children in Alaska.

The colony flourishes under Baranov; he serves as chief manager for 27 years, retiring at 71. Baranov dies in 1819 en route home to Russia.

1791: Grigorii Konovalov and 62 other hunters found St. Nicholas trading post at the mouth of the Kenai River. The Lebedev-Lastochkin Co. takes over the post and

gains control of most of the fur trade in Cook Inlet.

1791-95: George Vancouver, who twice sailed with Cook, leads a North Pacific scientific expedition for Britain and becomes the first European to report sighting high mountains (later named Mount McKinley and Mount Foraker) from Cook Inlet. Detailed charts of the Alaska and British Columbia coasts prepared by Vancouver's men are relied on by mariners for decades.

1793: Baranov oversees construction of a St. Paul harbor post; the city of Kodiak eventually develops there.

The first Russian-built ship in Alaska, the three-masted Phoenix, is constructed at Voskrensenskoye, or Resurrection, near present-day Seward.

September 1794: Kodiak becomes the center of Russian Orthodoxy in Alaska after a mission of 10 monks arrives from Okhotsk.

1795: Juvenal, among the original monks sent to Alaska, dies near Quinhagak in an unexplained attack by Natives.

July 1795: Shelikhov dies suddenly in Irkutsk, possibly of an intestinal malady.

1796: Intended as an agricultural settlement, New Russia is established at present-day Yakutat.

July 1799: Paul I charters the Russian American Co., a reorganization of the Shelikhov companies, giving it monopoly status in Alaska's fur trade. Baranov becomes the company's chief manager and establishes Archangel Michael post near present-day Sitka.

Alaska Natives are required to sell furs only to the Russian American Co.

Company posts ultimately extend as far north as Nulato on the Yukon River and south to Fort Ross, Calif., playing a key role in the settlement of Alaska and the Pacific Northwest through 1867.

July 1, 1802: Tlingits sack the Russian fort on Baranof Island; some accounts say 20 Russians and 130 Aleuts are killed. Tlingits are driven out in 1804 with help from cannon fire from the Russian navy ship Neva. Russians build a fort at a new site, Novoarkhangelsk (New Archangel), known today as Sitka.

1803: Baranov furnishes the American vessel O'Cain with 20 ocean-worthy baidarkas and 40 Natives to pursue sea otters in California. Supplying Alaska Native hunters to a foreign ship becomes common Russian practice.

1803-06: Russia's first round-the-world voyage is completed under Capt. Ivan Kruzenshtern and naval officer Iurii Lisianskii. Alaska's Cape Krusenstern on the Chukchi Sea is named for the captain who retired as an admiral; Lisianski strait and inlet north of Baranof Island are named for Lisianskii.

1805: Yakutat Tlingit attack New Russia; the post is not reestablished.

1806: The Russian American Co. ship Juno arrives at San Francisco Bay, marking the first voyage from Sitka to Spanish California. Nikolai Rezanov, a Russian American Co. official, successfully bargains with Spanish officials for foodstuffs desperately needed at Sitka.

1808: New Archangel replaces Kodiak as the administrative center of Russian America, becoming known for gala balls and receptions hosted by aristocratic naval officers who would succeed Baranov.

The Russian government orders Baranov to end forced, unpaid labor of Alaska Natives. Russians and Natives alike are inoculated against smallpox.

1808: Sitka's first Russian Orthodox church is built.

November 1811: Baranov dispatches Ivan Kuskov and the ship Chirikov to California with a crew of Russian and Aleut workers to found Ross Office, about 75 miles north of San Francisco. The fort is sold in 1841.

1816: Russian mariner Otto von Kotzebue arrives at the northwest Alaska Native village that today bears his name.

1818: Baranov is replaced by naval officer Leontii Gagemeister (Ludwig von Hagemeister), for whom a Bristol Bay island and strait are named.

1818-20: The Russian American Co. sends traders into Alaska's interior in search of furbearers. Russians sail from Cook Inlet to establish Fort Alexander at the mouth of the Nushagak River to support the expansion.

An Alaska census on Jan. 1, 1819, shows nearly 400 Russians, 250 Creoles and 8,000 Natives.

1820: The first medical doctor, Vasilii Volkov, arrives at Sitka; the first hospital is built one year later.

1821: The Russian American Co. is granted a second 20-year charter. The government tries to stop foreign ships from trading in Alaska waters.

1824: The Rev. Ioann Veniaminov, who would be elevated in 1840 as Bishop Innocent and canonized St. Innocent in 1979, arrives at Unalaska as a Russian Orthodox missionary.

An accomplished craftsman, observer of the natural world and linguist who delivered his sermons in Aleut, Veniaminov wins Native converts by respecting their traditions. His *Notes on the Islands of the Unalaska District* is an unparalleled compilation of Aleut traditions.

Veniaminov becomes leader of the church in 1868 as Metropolitan of Moscow,

The Holy Transfiguration of Our Lord Russian Orthodox Church in Ninilchik on the Kenai Peninsula stands as a reminder today of Alaska's Russian influence. (Chlaus Lotscher)

holding the post until his death in 1879.

1824: The United States and Russia agree by treaty to a boundary between their claims at 54 degrees 40' N. The line today marks the southern boundary of Alaska.

1825: A treaty between Russia and England sets the boundary between their claims at the 141st meridian and along the crest of the Coast Mountains. The line is Alaska's eastern border today.

1826: Sailing the H.M.S. Blossom, Capt. Frederick Beechey arrives at Point Hope on the Chukchi Sea then continues north to Point Barrow.

1828: The Rev. Iakov Netsvetov, Alaska's first Creole Orthodox priest, establishes a church at Atka in the Aleutian Islands.

1830: Ferdinand Wrangell (Vrangell in Russian), for whom a Southeast Alaska town is named, becomes Russian American Co. governor, the company's designation for its top official after 1821. Elisabeth Wrangell accompanies her husband to Sitka, the first governor's wife to do so, and interjects civility into the frontier town.

1833: St. Michael Redoubt is built on the east side of St. Michael Island in Norton Sound.

Nikolai Petrovich Rezanov, (1764-1807), Grigorii Shelikhov's son-in-law, was instrumental in the success of the Russian American Co. His skill at obtaining food and supplies from the Spanish in California kept Russian colonists from starving in New Archangel. (Alaska State Library, PCA 20-82)

1834: At Wrangell's request, Andrei Glazunov leads an ambitious winter expedition in the Yukon River area.

In Southeast Alaska, Russians establish Fort Dionysius at the mouth of the Stikine River near present-day Wrangell.

1835: Russians block the Dryad, a Hudson's Bay Co. ship, from traveling up the Stikine to establish a trading post in British territory. Construction of a new British post becomes unnecessary after 1839 when the Hudson's Bay Co. leases Southeast Alaska lands from Russia.

1835: French and American whalers reach the Gulf of Alaska to hunt right whales valued for blubber rendered into lamp oil. Yankee whaling off Alaska would prosper for the next several decades, prompting hostile exchanges between Russian and U.S. governments.

1836-42: A smallpox epidemic breaks out; Alaska Natives are vaccinated.

1838: Kolmakovskii Redoubt is established on the Kuskokwim River.

1839: Fort Dionysius and Russian holdings on the Southeast Alaska mainland are leased to the Hudson's Bay Co. for 10 years in exchange for provisions.

Alaska's population is estimated at 8,070, including some 800 Russians.

1839-49: Naturalist Il'ia Voznesenskii undertakes a scientific expedition to California and Alaska for the Russian Academy of Sciences.

1840: Arvid Etholen, a Russian naval academy trained explorer of Finnish descent, becomes governor of Russian America. Etolin Island in Southeast Alaska is named for him.

1841: A Russian blockhouse built at the Yukon River site of Nulato is rebuilt after being destroyed by Natives.

1841: In California, John Sutter buys Fort Ross.

Sitka's first Lutheran services are held.

Russian Orthodox missionaries are dispatched to Nushagak; Creoles are qualified for Orthodox priesthood.

1842: Sitka's Russian Bishop's House is completed.

1842: Naval officer Lavrentii Zagoskin explores the Yukon River region including the Koyukuk River and middle and lower Kuskokwim River. Zagoskin collects natural history and takes notes on inhabitants. Zagoskin's classic book on his Russian America expeditions is published in 1848.

1844: Nicholas I signs a third charter for the Russian American Co.

1844-48: St. Michael's Cathedral, with a belfry clock made by Veniaminov, is built in Sitka.

1845: American whalers begin hunting bowhead in the Bering Sea and Arctic Ocean. More than 50 whaling ships a year ply the waters through the 1850s.

1845: The Native village of Ikogmiut is home to the Russian Orthodox Mission on the Yukon, known as Kwikpak Mission. The mission, which serves the Kuskokwim and Yukon river area, is headed by the Rev. Iakov Netsvetov. Despite periodic resistance, Russian Orthodoxy eventually is embraced by Alaska Natives especially at Kodiak, Sitka, Atka, Unalaska, Nushagak, St. Michael, Russian Mission, Kenai and the Pribilof Islands.

An Orthodox seminary and school opens in Sitka.

1847: Hudson's Bay Co. establishes a trading post at Fort Yukon, near the confluence of the Yukon and Porcupine rivers, knowing the terrain is Russian-held. Russian explorer Ruf Serebrennikov leads an expedition into Southcentral Alaska's Copper River area; the group is killed by Indians.

1847-52: Geologist Petr Doroshin surveys minerals on the Kenai Peninsula, around Cook Inlet and on Unga Island. Coal mining in Kachemak Bay begins in 1855.

1849: The colony begins exporting ice from Kodiak and Sitka to San Francisco.

Feb. 15, 1851: The Russian post at Nulato is sacked by Koyukuk River Natives, 53 die. The Nulato massacre, as the surprise attack was called, claims Lt. John J. Barnard, a

Catherine II, (1729-1796), empress of Russia for 34 years in the late 18th century, was an enthusiastic proponent of exploration and trade but insisted that the days of the huge colonial monopolies were passed. (Alaska State Library, PCA 01-3659)

British naval officer whose Nulato grave becomes a Yukon River landmark until it is lost to the elements.

1852: Sitka-area Natives kill 40 Stikine Natives arriving at Sitka for a council with Russians.

1852: Russian American Co. governor Mikhail Teben'kov supervises the compilation of maps and hydrographic data for an "Atlas of the Northwest Coast of America." Drawn and engraved at Sitka, the atlas is printed in St. Petersburg.

1853: The first of several settlements on the Kenai Peninsula is established to accommodate Russians who choose not to return home after completing duty in the colony. Present-day Seldovia and Ninilchik grew from these settlements.

1853-56: The Russian American and Hudson's Bay companies are neutral during the Crimean War, in which Russia is de-feated by Britain, France and allies. War expenses prompt interest in cost saving and in 1857, Grand Duke Konstantin, brother of the czar, encourages sale of Russian America to the United States. Negotiations are sidetracked as the U.S. Civil War looms.

1861: The San Francisco-based cod fleet begins voyages north to the Shumagin Islands for commercial fishing.

1864: Prince Dmitrii Maksutov becomes the last governor of Russian America.

1865: The Western Union Telegraph Expedition, a private undertaking, ventures to western Alaska. The project disbands in 1867, one year after the success of an Atlantic cable, but plays a role in Alaska's purchase through the scientific information collected.

1866: Russia's Washington ambassador, Baron Eduard Stoeckl, initiates negotiations with U.S. Secretary of State William H. Seward for Alaska's purchase; the treaty is finalized in 1867.

Russia is paid $7.2 million, about two pennies an acre. The exchange is completed at Sitka on Oct. 18, 1867, and most Russians return home. Land claims of Alaska Natives are acknowledged by the treaty but remain unresolved until 1971 when Congress adopts the Alaska Native Claims Settlement Act . ■

Consolidation and Expansion:
The Russian American Co.

By Katherine Arndt

In July 1797 a number of the Irkutsk merchants active in the Alaska fur trade, including the heirs of Grigorii Shelikhov, merged their interests to form a single company. Just over a year later the merger received imperial confirmation and the firm incorporated under the name "United American Company." Under its Act of Incorporation, merchants not part of the original merger were allowed to join on the condition that their assets be paid into the company's general capital in exchange for shares. Though merchants were not forced to join and competition was technically still possible, none of the would-be competitors had deep enough pockets to resist for long.

The combined assets of the new company were impressive. Where numerous small companies had operated in earlier decades, there were now three semiautonomous districts operated out of a single head office in Irkutsk. The Unalaska district, headed by Irkutsk merchant Emel'ian Larionov, extended from the Fox Islands east to the Alaska Peninsula and north to Bering Strait. Besides a company office

and storage facilities at the settlement on Captains Harbor (Captains Bay) on Unalaska Island, the district had work parties on the Pribilof Islands and at various Native villages in the Fox Islands. The Atka Co., administered out of Okhotsk, took in all the islands lying west of the Unalaska district: the Andreanof, Rat, Near, Commander and Kurile island groups. It maintained a small party on Atka and neighboring islands and a detachment on Urup Island in the Kuriles. The Kodiak district, run by Aleksandr Baranov, encompassed everything to the east of the Unalaska district. By far the largest of the districts, it included an administrative center at Pavlovskaia Harbor (present-day Kodiak); outposts at Kenai, English Bay (present-day Nanwalek) and

FACING PAGE: *Sitka, on the west side of Baranof Island, is home today to about 9,000 people. During Russian rule in the 1800s, Sitka was known as the "Paris of the Pacific," and offered a lively cultural scene. It was then the largest city on the continent's west coast and an affluent commercial center. (Fred Hirschmann)*

Nuchek; a new settlement near Yakutat; and small work parties at a number of Native settlements in the Kodiak archipelago.

In July 1799 Emperor Paul I made official what, for all practical purposes, already existed in fact. By decree, he granted the United American Co., renamed the "Russian-American Company under Highest Protection of His Imperial Majesty," a 20-year monopoly over all resources on the northwestern coast of North America from 55 degrees N latitude to Bering Strait and beyond, plus the Aleutians, Kuriles and other islands. Merchants who had failed to join the united company no longer had a right to compete with it in those regions.

The new company also gained the right to explore and occupy newly discovered lands in the name of Russia, to establish settlements where needed, and to engage in commerce with all nearby powers (upon their consent and imperial confirmation). Moreover, Russian military commanders were authorized to use their forces to support the company's needs. In return, the company's managing body (Glavnoe Pravlenie, variously translated as Main Administration, Main Office and Board of Directors) was to report on all its activities directly to the emperor. From its beginning, the Russian American Co. was not only a business enterprise, but a means through which to consolidate Russian interests in northwestern North America and hinder foreign expansion into the region.

Throughout much of its existence, two basic considerations guided the Russian American Co.'s decisions concerning where in its vast territory to concentrate its attention and resources at any given time: (1) where were the most marketable species of furbearers to be found in greatest abundance, and (2) where were foreign, primarily British and American, competitors threatening its monopoly? In 1799, both those concerns pointed the company toward the Alexander Archipelago in Southeastern Alaska. There, sea otters were still to be found in some abundance. There, too, British and American vessels, engaged in the maritime fur trade, freely cruised waters that lay well within the territory reserved for the company.

Expansion into Southeast Alaska

The challenge of moving into Southeastern Alaska fell to the Russian American Co.'s Kodiak district. As longtime manager for Grigorii Shelikhov in that same district, Aleksandr Baranov had already laid the groundwork for expansion in that direction. In 1795 he had reconnoitered the hunting potential of Sitka Sound while his associate, James Shields, traded at Bucareli Bay and examined the coast from there north. The following year he had dispatched an Aleut hunting party to Lituya Bay, where they caught some 1800 sea otters. The party's escort, Shields, then proceeded to Sitka Sound for further explorations and to establish relations with local Natives. And in 1797 and 1798, his Aleut parties had successfully hunted and traded in the vicinity of Sitka Sound itself. Based on this promising start, Baranov was determined to establish a settlement in the area as soon as possible.

This monument at Grigorii Shelikhov's gravesite at Irkutsk stands outside Znamenskii Cathedral. Shelikhov died in Irkutsk in 1795, five years after he appointed Aleksandr Baranov manager of his interests in North America. According to historian Richard A. Pierce, this appointment may be Shelikhov's greatest achievement. (Penny Rennick)

In those days, it took six months or longer for news to reach the colony from European Russia. Consequently, Baranov was unaware of the Russian American Co.'s formation when he set out for Sitka

The Siberian port of Okhotsk described in 1788 by Martin Sauer, expedition secretary for English Lt. Joseph Billings, included dreary dwellings, badly stocked stores and difficult weather. The town subsequently became the most important Russian port for trade with the "east." (Anchorage Museum of History and Art)

Sound in the summer of 1799 to choose a site for the proposed settlement. He personally spent the winter of 1799-1800 overseeing a construction crew of 30 and an Aleut party of 50 (including six women) who procured food and performed other necessary work.

Despite chronic shortages of personnel and supplies the new post, named in honor of Archangel Michael but known today as Old Sitka, enjoyed considerable success in its first two seasons of hunting and trade. Still, the settlement's position was precarious. Both the Tlingit, the resident Native people who owned the region's resources, and the British and American vessel masters who traded with them viewed the company's activities as a potential threat to their own economic interests. The Tlingit provoked a number of minor confrontations, testing the settlement's vulnerability, while British and American vessels, anchored within sight of the post, exchanged guns, powder and other goods for Tlingit sea otter skins.

Old Sitka came to an end in June of 1802, destroyed in a Tlingit attack. A British vessel, under

This map shows the paths of Vitus Bering's voyages, as well as a faint indication of the outline of present-day Alaska, "land of which there are hints," according to the text below the words "Mer D' Anadir." (#G9236 S12 1754, Alaska and Polar Regions Archives, Rasmuson Library, University of Alaska Fairbanks)

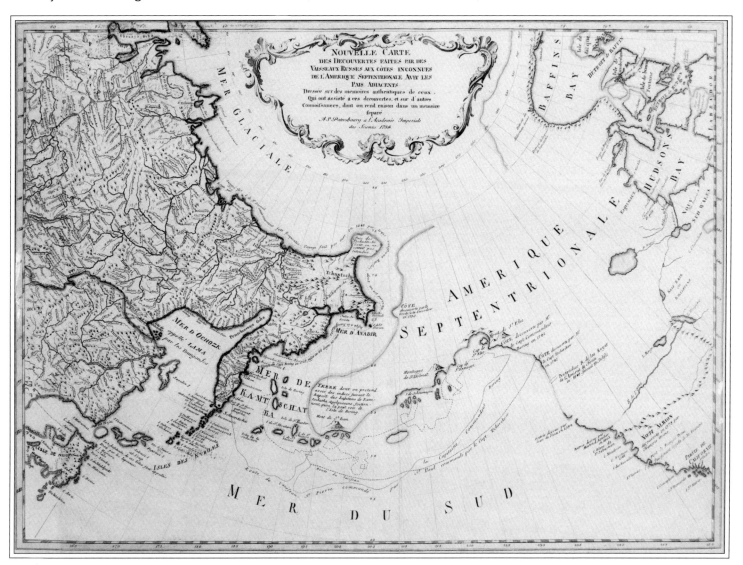

Capt. Henry Barber, and an American vessel, under Capt. John Ebbets, happened upon the scene several days later and managed to rescue 23 survivors (or

32 — accounts differ). Barber transported them to Kodiak, where he yielded them to Baranov in exchange for a sizable ransom. An Aleut party returning to Old Sitka from a hunt also fell victim to the Tlingit. Its few survivors made their way to the Russians' Yakutat settlement. Their arrival, and that of another large party which had been forewarned of the danger and turned back, averted a similar assault on Yakutat itself.

The attacks were reportedly the joint effort of

In the first year of Russian expansion to the Pribilofs and Aleutians, hunters killed more than 40,000 fur seals and traded their fur in Russia and China for other goods. Historical accounts report the Chinese paid "astronomical" sums for top-quality pelts. (Harry M. Walker)

Natives from all over Southeastern Alaska, instigated by the southern Tlingit and Haida and encouraged, perhaps even aided, by British and American traders. If their goal was to drive the Russians from the region, they were temporarily successful. It was two years before Baranov could muster the resources to reestablish a presence on Sitka Sound.

Accounts of the retaking of Sitka vary in their details, but the main points are as follows: Baranov returned to the area in September 1804, backed by four vessels of the colonial fleet and the ship Neva, under Capt. Iurii Lisianskii, which had recently arrived from European Russia with supplies. The Tlingit, long expecting retaliation, had already abandoned their village and withdrawn to a fort on a part of the bay so shallow that the Russian vessels found it difficult to approach. The Russians took possession of a steep-sided hill (Castle Hill) at the abandoned village site and attempted to negotiate the right to establish a post there. When negotiations failed, they tried instead to storm the Tlingit fort, but were repulsed. The next day the Neva opened fire. The Tlingit sued for peace, offering hostages and releasing some Aleut prisoners, but refused to give up their fort. After several more days of siege, however, they slipped away to Chatham Strait, abandoning Sitka Sound to the Russians. His way clear, Baranov immediately set about building a fortified settlement of his own, named Novoarkhangelsk (New Archangel, present-day Sitka).

Running the Colonies

The Russian American Co. underwent many organizational changes in its initial years of operation. Its Main Office was almost immediately transferred from the Siberian town of Irkutsk to the

Scientist Georg W. Steller, aboard Vitus Bering's ship in 1741, described with a naturalist's eye the playfulness, beauty and cunning of the sea otter. The sea otter has the densest fur of any mammal; its underfur of inch-long fibers averages 300,000 hairs per square inch. (Harry M. Walker)

Russian capital, St. Petersburg. Management in the colonies was made more hierarchical — Baranov was elevated to the newly created position of chief manager and the company establishment at Kodiak became the colonial capital. But in recognition of the continued importance of Southeastern Alaska as the region most threatened by foreign interlopers, the seat of colonial administration moved to Sitka a short time later, in 1808.

In these early years company settlements

FACING PAGE: *The Kamchatka Peninsula in eastern Russia was the jumping-off point for mariners facing stormy seas on their way to find North America. (Ernest Manewal)*

BELOW: *This painting by John Webber (1808?) shows the narta, or sledge, used for overland travel and transport of goods between Russian ports and interior posts. Vitus Bering used sled dogs to transport goods across the Kamchatka Peninsula in the winter of 1727-28, when he feared that sailing his ship Fortuna around the tip of Kamchatka would be disastrous due to stormy seas. (Anchorage Museum of History and Art)*

continually suffered supply problems. Most goods sent from European Russia were transported overland to Okhotsk, then by sea to the colonies. Items were often pilfered or heavily damaged in transit, and freight rates were prohibitive. For greater efficiency, the Main Office experimented with sending goods around the world by sea from Russia's Baltic port of Kronstadt. The results were promising, but the company did not yet have the means to finance such voyages on an annual basis.

Baranov found an alternative in the American

Beginning in the 1700s, Russian mariners anchored at Captains Harbor (Captains Bay) near the present-day community of Unalaska. As fur-trading increased, a settlement, occupied intermittently, evolved around an observatory tent (1), Aleut yurts (barabaras) (3), Russian barracks (4), and on a small hill, the gravesites of Russian navigators (2). Naval officer Gavriil Sarychev's ship, Slava Rossii (Glory of Russia), lies offshore. (Drawing by Luka Voronin, artist with Billings-Sarychev Expedition)

vessels calling at the colony's main port, Kodiak before 1808 and Sitka thereafter. He struck various deals with the American skippers, sometimes even lending them parties of Aleuts for joint hunting expeditions to far-off California. This trade reached a volume of thousands of dollars annually, for which Baranov obtained food, manufactured goods, and occasionally the very vessels aboard which the goods were delivered.

Old Russian Cannons Unalaska, Alaska

Though this method of supply was cheaper and more reliable than anything the company itself could offer, it was in one respect self-defeating. By 1810, sea otter catches in Southeastern Alaska had noticeably declined due to overhunting and the trade increasingly focused on less profitable land mammal pelts. British vessels had already abandoned the region, but competition among American traders remained stiff. For a number of them, the ability to sell foodstuffs and manufactured goods in Sitka at a healthy profit meant that they could still afford to spend most of their time trading with the Tlingit despite decreasing fur returns.

Russian seamen used cannons as defense artillery, but also as a way of communication between companion ships when stormy weather hampered visibility. Thirty-two years after the United States purchased Alaska, this collection was photographed at Unalaska. (#310, J.N. Wyman Collection, Anchorage Museum of History and Art)

Permanent structures housed Sitka residents in the early 1800s after Baranov moved the colonial capital there from Kodiak. (#C0024, Alaska and Polar Regions Archives, Rasmuson Library, University of Alaska Fairbanks)

Setting Boundaries

The company was unsuccessful in its early petitions to the Russian government to stop foreign vessels from trading with Natives in Southeastern Alaska. The government did not wish to press the matter diplomatically, and was unwilling to give military powers to a purely mercantile organization. The company then tried to discourage the intruders through economic measures, instructing Baranov and his successors to curtail their purchase of supplies from vessels that called at Sitka, but the problem persisted.

It was not until renewal of the company's 20-year charter came under discussion that the Russian government was ready to address the matter of foreign encroachment on its colonial possessions. The faction arguing that the Russian navy should play a larger role in company, and colonial, management won its point. The second charter, approved in 1821, contained a clause requiring the chief manager be chosen from among officers of the navy, thus excluding the merchant class from the highest position in colonial administration. At the same time an imperial decree was issued prohibiting all foreign vessels from landing on or approaching within 100 Italian (nautical) miles of the shores of Russia's possessions and from conducting any trade with the Natives there. A naval sloop already en route to the colony was ordered to patrol the coast for violators.

The decree of 1821 elicited immediate protests both from the colony and from the United States and Great Britain. Residents of the colony faced real hardship as managers scrambled to find other sources of supply. Fortunately, the prohibition did not extend to the company's Ross settlement in California, and trade with American vessels there and in Hawaii partially offset the anticipated shortages. For their part, the American and British governments were less disturbed over a potential loss in commerce than over the decree's definition of the southern boundary of the closed area: 51 degrees N.

The Russian government, finding it politically inconvenient to antagonize Great Britain at that time, entered into negotiations which resulted in the conventions of 1824 with the United States and 1825 with Great Britain. The southern boundary of Russian possessions on the Northwest Coast was set at 54 degrees 40' N. From that parallel, and north to Mount St. Elias, the eastern boundary of the colony was to extend no more than 10 marine leagues (about 30 miles) inland from tidewater. From Mount St. Elias north to the Arctic Ocean, the eastern boundary followed the 141st meridian. Americans were granted the right to trade and fish freely in colonial waters for a period of 10 years. The British were granted the right, in perpetuity, of free navigation on all rivers and streams that crossed the Russian coastal strip from British territory in what is today Canada.

The Russian American Co. protested that the government had legalized the very practices that had damaged its trade, but to no avail. In the colony, however, disappointment was tempered with

When Vitus Bering's crew ran aground on Bering Island in 1741, Georg W. Steller wrote of the bold behavior of blue foxes: "If we lay down as if sleeping they sniffed at our nostrils to see whether we were dead or alive." (Julie E. Sprott)

A Native man and his son pose near a portion of old Fort St. Michael that housed a cannon. Lt. Mikhail D. Teben'kov chose the site and supervised building of the post in 1833. The settlement was the northernmost outpost of Russian Orthodoxy and trade. (#58-1026-2291 N, Charles Bunnell Collection, Alaska and Polar Regions Archives, University of Alaska Fairbanks)

relief. The conventions reopened the port of Sitka to international trade.

Refocus on the North and West

While Southeastern Alaska remained at the forefront of company concerns about competition and boundaries through 1825, it was clear by the mid-1810s that new sources of fur revenues would have to be sought in other regions. The sea otter populations that had attracted the company to Southeast were already in decline, and sharp competition, combined with lingering Tlingit resentment against the Russian intruders, kept much of the remaining sea otter catch out of Russian hands. The region's growing trade in land mammal furs offered little hope, for it was developing along the same channels, bypassing the Russians. The greatest potential for future profits lay to the north and west, in the virtually untapped mainland interior and in the overhunted Aleutian, Pribilof and Commander islands.

Colonial managers turned first to the region north of Bristol Bay, a land of myriad lakes and streams long rumored to abound with beaver. In 1818 an expedition led by Petr Korsakovskii explored the lower reaches of the major rivers flowing into the bay from the north and ascended the Kvichak River to Lakes Iliamna and Clark. From there, one detachment continued north, possibly as far as the Kuskokwim River. The explorers returned with favorable reports of rich fur resources and of a Native population eager to trade. Wasting no time, the company established a post at the mouth of the Nushagak River the following summer with orders to develop the trade of that drainage.

In 1819 Creole Afanasii Klimovskii led an expedition up the Copper River from Prince William

Sound. In the company's early years, several parties had penetrated this region in unsuccessful searches for sources of the mica and copper known to come from there. This time the goal was to gather information on trade routes and fur resources. The results were sufficiently encouraging for the company to place a small trading station a fair distance upriver, slightly below the mouth of the Chitina, about 1821 or 1822. Administered and supplied out of the company post at Nuchek, it was never a large establishment, nor did a large Native settlement spring up around it. Nor, for that matter, did it ever realize its potential as a forward base from which to launch further explorations. It did, however, funnel a good number of furs to the company during the many years of its existence.

Also the object of attention at this time was the whole west coast of the Alaska mainland, from Bristol Bay to the Arctic Ocean. Russian naval expeditions had visited the region on more than one occasion, continuing a long tradition of arctic exploration. In 1821 and 1822, the Russian American Co. itself sent an expedition, two vessels under the command of Vasilii S. Khromchenko and A. Adolf Etholen. Geographical discovery was but a minor goal. Much more important from the company's perspective were new trade contacts with coastal inhabitants and any information that could be gathered concerning the mainland interior. In this the expedition was quite successful. Besides making contact and conducting modest trade with Natives in the vicinity of Golovnin Bay, it returned

This Russian chapel bell at Fort Ross, California, where Russian traders hoped to nurture agricultural abundance, still survives after many years of travel and hardship. (Kathy Doogan)

with information on an active trade between Natives of Alaska and Asia across Bering Strait, a trade that was channeling furs from Alaska's interior to the fur markets of Siberia.

Distracted by the supply difficulties that followed the closure of colonial waters in 1821, by international negotiations to settle colonial boundaries, and by efforts to implement new

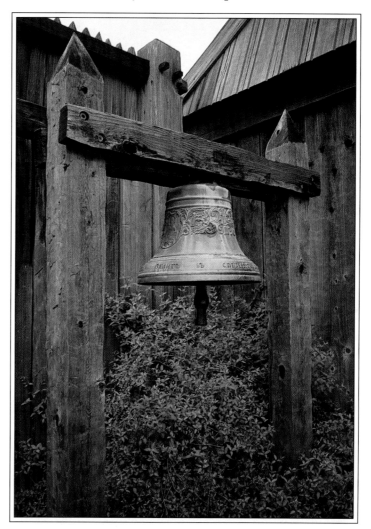

requirements contained in its second charter, the
company did not immediately have the means to
follow up on its initial progress in developing the
mainland trade. It did, however, institute measures
to enhance its returns from the somewhat neglected
western islands.

The chief obstacle to company profits in the
Aleutian, Pribilof and Commander islands was
depletion of furbearer populations, a legacy of the
days of fierce competition among the many
independent fur companies. In those times there
was no incentive for conservation. If one company
left an area unhunted to let animal populations
recover, there was no guarantee that it would reap
the reward before a rival moved in. But now there
were no competitors in that region. The future
sustainability of the fur resource rested fully in the
hands of the Russian American Co.

The company's earliest conservation measures
focused on the fur seal. Beginning in 1804, when
the colonies had an oversupply of poorly processed
fur seal skins and seal herds were in noticeable
decline, a four-year hunting closure was instituted
on the Pribilof Islands. Thereafter, the annual take
was to be restricted, but local managers often broke
the restriction to meet Baranov's demand for skins
with which to purchase supplies. From the 1820s
through 1867, periodic restrictions or outright
hunting closures were more successfully observed.
During these years, similar hunting closures were

also occasionally enacted for fox, sea lion and other animals, as the need arose.

Conservation measures focusing on sea otters came into official use only in the late 1830s, when a hunting rotation system was implemented. No hunting area was to be exploited two years in succession. It was reported, however, that such rotation had long since been observed by local Aleut leaders, who had some say in where the hunt was to be conducted each year.

From the late 1820s onward, the company also tried to enhance the region's returns by stocking uninhabited islands with desirable species of fox. So as not to disrupt local subsistence, managers were to choose islands not used by the Aleuts for bird hunting and egg gathering, because the foxes might destroy that resource. Once an island was stocked with several breeding pairs, it was left untouched until fox population reached a level that could sustain a harvest.

All these practices were also extended to the Atka district, the administration of which was transferred from Okhotsk to Sitka in 1825. Through such measures, the company was able to achieve and maintain a fairly steady, if unspectacular, fur yield from the western districts of the colony for years.

ABOVE RIGHT: *Merchant and customer discuss a price for blue jeans in a Petropavlovsk market in the Russian Far East. Trade between Russia and America has expanded greatly since the time of the first Russian explorations of North American shores. (Ernest Manewal)*

RIGHT: *Stemming from the earliest days of Russian Orthodoxy at Kodiak, the tradition of blessing the fleet is perpetuated today during the King Crab Festival. (Harry M. Walker)*

New Threats to the Southeast

With the company's attention shifting to the fur resources of the north and west, Sitka was no longer necessarily the best location for the colonial capital. In terms of supplying the company's existing and projected posts, and even in terms of hospitality of surrounding Native peoples, it made much more sense to transfer the capital back to a more centrally located site such as Kodiak. The company's Main Office authorized such a move in 1822.

Considerable construction was needed at Kodiak before it could house all the personnel, offices and support facilities required for the administrative center. For lack of materials and skilled labor, the work commenced only in 1828 and went slowly. In 1832, however, all plans for the move were abruptly canceled. By then, Southeastern Alaska had assumed new importance as a buffer against foreign encroachment on the colony, this time by the Hudson's Bay Co.

The seeds of this problem lay in certain provisions of the boundary-setting conventions of 1824 and 1825. Only a handful of American traders took advantage of their 10-year right under the convention to trade in colonial waters, but they were very active. Their continued profits from the sale of supplies at Sitka made it possible for them to pay higher prices than their competition in the coastal fur trade. With sea otters very rare, they dealt primarily in land mammal furs brought to the coast by Native middlemen. The source of many of those furs was the interior of what is now British Columbia, the territory of the Hudson's Bay Co.

One of the Hudson's Bay Co.'s strategies to intercept the furs was to establish a chain of posts between its Fort Vancouver on the Columbia River and the southern boundary of Russian territory. The last link in the chain was to be a post within British territory up the Stikine River, the mouth of which

LEFT: *The Russian double eagle coat-of-arms marks this cannon at Sitka. About 40 cannons, many salvaged from old ships, surrounded the Russian Governor's House on Castle Hill overlooking Sitka's harbor. (Ernest Manewal)*

FACING PAGE: *St. George the Great Martyr Russian Orthodox Church at St. George is testimony to the heritage left behind by Russian influences. The Russian American Co. sent Aleuts to the Pribilof Islands to hunt sea otters and fur seals. The Rev. Ioann Veniaminov, first Russian Orthodox priest assigned to the Unalaska parish, often wrote in his journals of the warm welcome he received when visiting Aleuts in the Pribilofs. (Dan Parrett)*

Early Russian rubles consisted of seal and walrus skin, but the Russian American Co. obtained a new form — paper. Various governors of Sitka had problems with paper notes fading and tearing too easily, and this lack of sturdy currency often hampered daily business transactions. (#98-15, Alaska State Museum)

lay in the Russian colony. The company intended to exercise British rights of navigation on rivers which crossed the colonial boundary, per the convention of 1825.

Rumors of the plan reached Russian colonial officials at Sitka. Fearing that the proposed post would adversely affect the Russian American Co.'s fur returns, Chief Manager Ferdinand P. Wrangel sought to stop it. His primary hope lay in another provision of the convention, whereby British vessels were allowed refuge and berthing at places occupied by Russian settlements only with the permission of the settlements' heads. He took immediate measures to assure that the Hudson's Bay Co. would encounter such a settlement near the Stikine River.

In the autumn of 1833 Wrangel ordered construction of Redoubt St. Dionysius (present-day Wrangell) on Wrangell Island, which lay on the approach to the Stikine's mouth. There was no opposition from the local Tlingit, for the company had been careful to court their good will and had purchased the right to use the fort site from a brother of the local chief. The 22-man post was completed and staffed just in time, in May 1834.

When the Hudson's Bay Co. vessel Dryad arrived off the mouth of the Stikine a month later, those aboard were indeed surprised to see a Russian post that had not been there a year earlier. Unable to sail up the river, they were forced to ask permission to anchor while they prepared to tow the vessel to their destination. Not only was permission refused by the Russians, but the local Tlingit voiced strong opposition to what they perceived as a threat to their role as middlemen in the trade between the coast and the continental interior. After a week of futile attempts to negotiate, the Dryad turned back.

The Hudson's Bay Co. sued for damages, claiming violation of the 1825 convention. In the prolonged negotiations that followed, the Russian government's interest in preserving good relations with Great Britain took precedence over its support for the company. Under the settlement reached in 1839, the Hudson's Bay Co. was permitted to lease exclusive rights to the Russian colony's mainland coastal strip, from Portland Canal to Cape Spencer, for a period of 10 years effective from June 1840. In exchange, the Russian American Co. was to receive annual rent of 2,000 land otter pelts, with the option to purchase more at a fixed price. The Hudson's Bay Co. also agreed to supply Sitka with food staples at predetermined prices and to transport Russian cargos at a fixed freight rate. The Russians retained exclusive rights to the remainder of Southeastern Alaska and to all sea otters taken anywhere in the region.

With commencement of its lease, the Hudson's Bay Co. occupied Redoubt St. Dionysius, renamed Fort Stikine, and built a new post, Fort Durham, at the mouth of the Taku River. It abandoned the latter in 1843 and Fort Stikine in 1849, but, under lease renewals, continued to send a trading vessel to the coast each summer. American traders who had continued to haunt the southern boundary of the territory even after expiration of their rights to cruise colonial waters found that their once-sure source of profit had dried up. Because of the new shipping and supply agreements with the Hudson's Bay Co., Sitka no longer had need of their cargoes, and they withdrew from the region entirely. That source of competition eliminated, the Hudson's Bay and Russian American cos. were able to set fur prices to their mutual benefit, and to the detriment of the Tlingit.

Pursuing the Northern Trade

While dealing with problems of sovereignty in Southeastern Alaska, the Russian American Co. was simultaneously seeking new sources of profit in the north. Based upon the explorations of the early 1820s, Chief Manager Petr E. Chistiakov decided to focus upon two areas: the headwaters of the Nushagak, Kuskokwim and Yukon rivers, then thought to lie close together; and the coast of Norton Sound. The former area boasted large

populations of beaver and land otter; the latter was visited by Native middlemen, the Aziiagmiut, active in the trade across Bering Strait.

The company's Nushagak post served as the base from which to launch explorations of the Nushagak and Kuskokwim drainages. In 1829 and 1830, Ensign Ivan I. Vasil'ev led expeditions into that region to explore the courses of the major rivers, collect information on Native populations, fur resources and trade, and to seek a promising location for a trading station. He penetrated as far as the middle course of the Kuskokwim and descended that river to the coast. Though he did not reach the Yukon drainage, he gathered

Russian-Americans used lead weights to measure vegetables and other goods in funts (pounds). (#IIIR69, Alaska State Museum)

enough information about trade patterns there to recommend Stuart Island in Norton Sound as a site for a new post.

Further explorations of the Kuskokwim region

Naval officer Iurii Lisianskii (1773-1837) surveyed "Cadiak" (Kodiak and neighboring islands) during his 1803-06 round-the-world voyage with Capt. Ivan Kruzenshtern (1770-1846). (File photo)

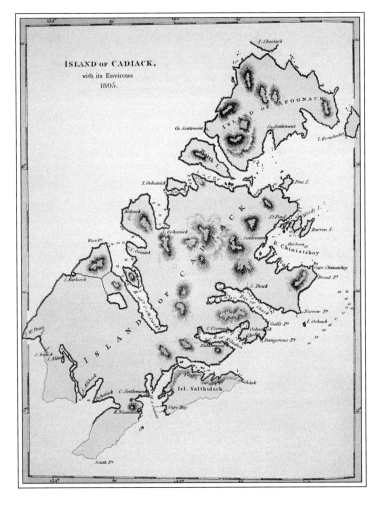

were entrusted to the company traders long resident at Nushagak: Fedor Kolmakov, his Creole son Petr, and the Creole Semen Lukin. In 1832 and 1833 Kolmakov senior led trade expeditions directly to the Native villages and camps of the Holitna and middle Kuskokwim rivers. At several places the party built small huts to serve as way stations, collection points and storage depots. With this groundwork in place, Kolmakov returned to his duties as head of the Nushagak post and entrusted development of the Kuskokwim trade to Semen Lukin, under whom it flourished. The major post of the region, Kolmakovskii Redoubt, was established on the middle Kuskokwim in 1841 at the site of one of Lukin's stations. Within a few years, it had succeeded Nushagak as the center of the company's trade in Southwestern Alaska.

Initial investigations of trade potential in the Norton Sound area were conducted from aboard ship. In 1830 a vessel under Lt. A. Adolf Etholen, who had been on a similar mission in the region a decade earlier, traded on an experimental basis at various stops on the Sound and the shores of the Bering Sea. His relative success, combined with Ensign Vasil'ev's recommendation of Stuart Island as the site for a company establishment, prompted the dispatch of a company vessel to those same waters in the three succeeding summers. Commanded by Lt. Mikhail D. Teben'kov, the expeditions were to trade, select a site for a post, and, in 1833, oversee establishment of Redoubt St. Michael just south of Stuart Island and slightly north of the mouth of the Yukon.

As had been the company's experience many years earlier when it first built a post in Southeastern Alaska, the Natives who controlled the region's trade did not welcome their presence. This time the results were not as deadly. In 1835

These Russian stamps celebrate the Russian American connection. Top: Ivan Kuskov, Aleksandr Baranov's chief assistant, chose the location of Fort Ross with military defense in mind. Center: Aleksandr Baranov was one of the co-founders of Sitka. Bottom: Grigorii Shelikhov established the first permanent Russian colony in Alaska on Kodiak Island. (Ernest Manewal)

a party working outside the redoubt walls was attacked by a number of Aziiagmiut, but escaped with one dead and seven wounded. The post redoubled its vigilance and thereafter maintained an uneasy peace with Native traders.

St. Michael was not ideally situated to dominate the region's trade, but its coastal location made it relatively easy to supply by seagoing vessel and it was a convenient base from which to extend explorations farther into the interior. Between 1833 and 1838, half a dozen small expeditions examined the lower Yukon drainage and various portages between the Yukon and the coast and between the Yukon and Kuskokwim drainages, collecting information on local trade routes. Based on their recommendations, small trading stations were established at Ikogmiut (present-day Russian Mission) in 1836 and at Nulato in 1839. The latter marked the northernmost extent of the Russian American Co.'s network of permanently staffed posts.

The company's most elaborate expedition into the Yukon-Kuskokwim region, which continued from autumn of 1842 through early summer of 1844, was entrusted to Lt. Lavrentii Zagoskin. His mission was to verify and tie together the geographical information collected by all previous expeditions there and then to push on into areas not yet explored. Zagoskin was also to collect detailed information on trade routes and the types of goods circulating in the trade. His exploration of unknown territory reached only about 100 miles up the Yukon beyond Nulato, but he did manage to integrate much of the existing information about the region and gather the trade information needed by the company to make its operations there more effective.

New Directions

By 1841, the Russian American Co.'s network of trading stations throughout Alaska was in place. Thereafter, growth of the take in furs depended on development of trade relations out of existing posts rather than establishment of new ones. Even when the Hudson's Bay Co. crossed the colony's eastern border to build Fort Yukon in 1847, the Russian American Co. did not mount a direct challenge. At

Alutiiqs in baidarkas paddle St. Paul Harbor while a Russian trading ship lies at anchor at what is now Kodiak. Iurii Lisianskii, an artist as well as navigator, painted this scene in 1804. Lisianskii's naval career included expeditious promotion through the Russian Naval Cadet Corps[o] and service in the British fleet where he called at Halifax, Nova Scotia and the West Indies. While recuperating in Halifax from yellow fever, he traveled to Boston and Philadelphia and met President George Washington. (File photo)

the time, the Russians lacked the means to dispatch a major expedition to confront that post, and when they did finally obtain reliable intelligence through a spy dispatched in the early 1860s, the British were already too well entrenched to be easily ousted. Instead, the Russians had to content themselves with trying to out-compete their rivals.

Outside of the north, from the late 1840s onward the company focused much of its effort on developing the colony's other resources: fish, timber, coal and ice. In large part this was an outgrowth of the new markets for colonial products that developed in the Pacific following the California gold rush. Old company establishments took on new functions as colonial managers tried to supply the markets' demands. The era of new settlement had passed. ■

Katherine Arndt, Ph.D., a researcher specializing in Russian America history, is affiliated with the Department of Anthropology, University of Alaska Fairbanks.

BELOW: *Land-based furbearers, such as this red fox, became an alternative to sea mammals in the Russian fur trade. As populations of fur seals and sea otters declined, trappers moved inland to find other sources of fur. (Mike Jones)*

LOWER RIGHT: *Artist Katherine Delaney Abrams captures the strategic location of the Russian Governor's House atop Castle Hill at Sitka. Although the Americans called the building Baranov's Castle, the chief manager did not live in this building, which was built in 1837 and burned in 1894. (#VA268, Alaska State Museum)*

The Russian Orthodox Inheritance in Alaska

By The Rev. Michael Oleksa

EDITOR'S NOTE: *More than 200 years after Orthodox clergy stepped ashore in Russian America, debate persists over the Spiritual Mission's motivation: Were the financially dependent clerics, essentially Russian American Co. employees, dispatched to pacify Native people? How then to reconcile the devotion the monk-priests inspired among generations of Aleut and Southwest Alaska Native converts? While the mission encouraged, educated and advanced Native people — introducing bilingualism in the colony — did it also take advantage of a "powerless" people, as some critics say? What is the Church's true legacy in Alaska?*

As the Rev. Michael J. Oleksa points out, early missions inspired saints and martyrs, teachers and priests; the Church offered a spiritual home to the colony's Creoles. In Alaska, many of their descendants are faithful still, a living testament to hope in the New World.

Beginnings: The Czar Is Far Away

Responding to the promises of merchant Grigorii Shelikhov to support clergy in Alaska, Catherine II issued an edict in 1793 to send Russian Orthodox priests and monks to the New World, where they would have primary responsibility for the education and moral guidance of Natives and Russians alike. Shelikhov, at work on the foundations of the Russian American Co., apparently had mixed motives in asking for priests. Scholars say the request may have been mere window dressing, as Shelikhov sought to further his company's status with Catherine; others say he hoped clerics would end the fur entrepreneurs' practice of baptizing Aleuts, reducing their effectiveness as hunters since baptized Natives became loyal to their godfathers exclusively.

But if his reasons remain murky after more than 200 years, the effect of Shelikhov's appeal is clear — a legacy of Orthodoxy in Alaska that flourishes

FACING PAGE: *The colorful, serene interior of St. George the Great Martyr Russian Orthodox Church, on St. George Island in the Pribilofs, is the antithesis of the foggy, windswept land surrounding it. (Fred Hirschmann)*

The Rev. Ioann Veniaminov, shown here as Metropolitan of Moscow, was sent to Unalaska in 1824. He later became Bishop Innocent, and for many years supervised a widespread diocese from his seat In Sitka. In 1979 he was canonized as a saint. (Photo by Tserkovnyi Vedomosti, courtesy of Barbara Sweetland Smith)

today and traces its start to 1794 with the arrival in Kodiak of the Spiritual Mission.

Monks from Konevitsa and Valaam volunteered to serve as missionary teachers on Kodiak and the Aleutian Islands, hiking across Russia from their monasteries on Lake Ladoga near Finland and sailing for North America from Okhotsk in summer 1794. The group of 11, including the priest-monk Ioasaf Bolotov and the monks Herman and Iuvenalii (Juvenal), both eventually canonized, arrived at St. Paul Harbor, Kodiak, in September. (A priest-monk is a monk who has been ordained a priest.) Though untrained in ethnography, anthropology or even formally in theology, the monks' walk across Siberia had uniquely prepared them for their new lives.

The men stayed nightly at outpost monasteries, founded among nomadic, shamanistic tribal people. If the monks were seeking to understand the missionary expansion of Eastern Christianity, the remote monasteries provided training that no text ever could: They learned, for instance, that Orthodox monks since the 14th century had passed on a tradition of studying local tribal languages and customs, devising alphabets and translating scripture. Early clerics also published books and established schools from the Ural Mountains to Kamchatka.

In Alaska, Shelikhov had professed humane treatment of Native people and an interest in educating them; in dispatches home, he said Russians lived in harmony with Alutiiq neighbors, many of whom Shelikhov claimed to personally have baptized at Three Saints Bay.

But word of mistreatment of the Natives under Shelikhov began reaching home and in 1804, the priest-monk Gideon undertook a two-year inspection of the colony on behalf of church administrators. Gideon noted the "personal insults" aimed at the missionaries by Russian American Co. employees. Hostilities, he said, "were the results of the prevailing attitude that 'God is in heaven, the czar is far away' and only Baranov was to be feared."

Forceful Agent of Change

Across northern Asia, Slavic and Native Siberians intermarried frequently, raising interracial, multilingual families. After crews from the Bering-Chirikov expedition returned with top-quality sea otter pelts, Siberians and Creoles stampeded for the Aleutian archipelago in handwrought boats. A half-century of free trade by *promyshlenniki* followed and boats began calling each summer at Attu, Atka and Unalaska. Traders offered buckets, blankets and beads in exchange for sea otter pelts, for which the Chinese paid top ruble.

With the publication in 1886 of H.H. Bancroft's *History of Alaska*, conventional scholarship has repeated the claim that Russian traders destroyed the population of Aleutian Natives, known as the Unangax, and enslaved survivors. But contemporary researchers — including work by Alaska-based authorities such as Lydia Black and Katherine Arndt, as well as my own studies — suggest other factors should be taken into account, including intertribal warfare and disease. The Unangax also endured frequent attacks from their traditional enemies some 600 miles to the east on Kodiak Island.

Some historians now credit Russian rule with putting down these skirmishes: "The suppression,

Bishop Veniaminov became so proficient in Aleut dialects that his summary of Christian doctrine, "The Way to the Heavenly Kingdom," was written in Aleut and later translated into Russian. (Alaska State Library)

and later the elimination, of internecine warfare between various Aleut groups that had resulted from the Russians' arrival (should) be noted," writes R. G. Liapunova in *Russia's American Colony* (1987). "Such strife included wars between the Aleuts and Alegmutes (Eskimos of the Bristol Bay coast) and the particularly cruel wars between the Aleuts and Koniags (Eskimos of Kodiak Island and the coast of the Alaska Peninsula in Shelikhov Bay, now known

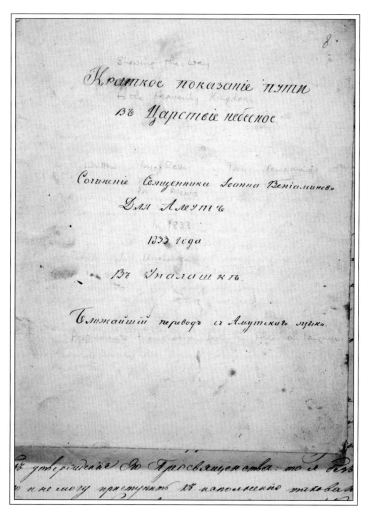

as Alutiiq) which resulted in the extermination of entire villages in some cases and in other cases the starvation of survivors who found themselves without providers following the siege."

Authorities differ about Native treatment or mistreatment at the hands of Russians, depending on the historical period. University of Alaska Anchorage anthropology professor Douglas W. Veltre says the colonial era can be divided into two periods, from 1741 to about 1800 and from 1800 to the Alaska Purchase of 1867; the earlier period, when Russian Orthodoxy became a "forceful agent of change" among the Aleut and Southwest Alaska Natives, is the more significant, Veltre states. Writing in *Russian America: The Forgotten Frontier* (1990), he notes: "Eventually, the church replaced most, if not all, of the precontact religious foundations of Native cultures.... By the end of the 1790s, Aleuts were no longer in control of their own lives."

Research also shows that some Natives were classified as Russian citizens when they either married Siberian Natives or Slavs or were recognized as "townsmen," an Imperial Russia social class with some education. Townsmen were the artisans and foremen of their day; the Russian American Co. turned to this class of men to fill its middle-management posts.

Exploitation of Native peoples may be traced to the demise of the free-trade period and the domination of the Russian American Co. heirs, whose goal was maximizing profits in the fur seal and sea otter trades. Among Shelikhov's legacies was the recruitment of Aleksandr Baranov, a veteran Siberian merchant, as the company's new manager in 1790. By the time missionaries arrived at Kodiak, Baranov's dictatorial rule was established, extracting tribute in furs and drafting hundreds of Kodiak men into company service. Referring to the Aleut, Baranov reported in 1791: "I didn't offend them in the slightest yet brought about their obedience."

Baranov's foreman, Ivan Kuskov, had a practice of approaching Native villages in the 1790s with a small cannon mounted on his boat, threatening destruction of the food supply if the community's hunters failed to meet their quota of pelts. Hundreds of Natives were forced to relocate to the Pribilof Islands to harvest the fur seals there. Other Natives

This Russian school in Unalaska was one of many built throughout Alaska during the Russian American period. Education was in the hands of Russian priests, whose duty it was to present reading, writing, geography, math and Church doctrine, as well as to translate at least one of the Gospels into a Native dialect and teach at least 50 people to read it. (Anchorage Museum of History and Art)

Artist Austin Deuel offers his interpretation of Russian Orthodox faithful leaving St. Michael's Cathedral. Sitka's first church was a small chapel built near the water in 1816. Items salvaged from the wreck of the ship Neva adorned the chapel. Twenty-five years later a new church known as St. Michael's Cathedral was begun closer to the center of town. That building burned on Jan. 2, 1966, but many adornments were saved and installed in the new building consecrated in 1976. (Courtesy of Bob White)

were dispatched to the Kenai Peninsula, Yakutat and Sitka, and as far south as Fort Ross and Hawaii; 200 Aleuts were resettled on Urup Island, in the Kurile Islands north of Japan.

Ioasaf, the Spiritual Mission's leader, appealed to the company to halt the injustice. When his demand was ignored, the priest sailed back to Siberia to present the case against Baranov to civil authorities. While in Russia, Ioasaf was ordained "bishop of Kodiak" with authority to put the Alaska colony in order, a goal the cleric did not live to achieve. In 1823, the ship returning him to Russian America sank, prompting some suspicion today of foul play.

Ioasaf had reported to church administrators that "Americans," as Native people were called, already had within their traditional mythologies the ethical basis of biblical tradition. For instance, they believed in an all-powerful creator and the common descent of all humans from an original couple. Ioasaf said Native teaching also embraced a moral code akin to the 10 Commandments and the groups even retold a tale of a catastrophic flood. "They accept baptism so readily that all their shaman robes have been torn up and burned," he wrote of Aleut converts in the winter of 1795. "Nobody can be turned away. We dare not sadden or insult anyone by turning them away."

The mission's early years were its most active when thousands of Natives were baptized, the first step in becoming a Christian. Authorities in St. Petersburg were troubled nonetheless by reports

Icon Painting

By Byron Birdsall

EDITOR'S NOTE: *Anchorage artist Byron Birdsall is among the finest observers of Alaska's landscape, capturing vintage scenes and modern cityscapes, Mount McKinley at daybreak, a solitary tree in winter.*

After a trip to the Aleutian Islands in 1984 to paint Russian Orthodox churches, Birdsall found himself drawn to devotional art known as icons (from the Greek word eikon, *to resemble.) "This was the first time I had seen the gilded religious paintings in their natural environment," he wrote in* Byron Birdsall's Alaska and Other Exotic Worlds *(1993). "I couldn't get them out of my mind."*

Soon the icons crowded his studio too and in 1986, Birdsall's series was exhibited at The Artique gallery in Anchorage. From the catalog, here are the artist's thoughts.

Traditional icon painting adheres to a strict discipline: The Virgin, for instance, is always shown in a limited variety of configurations. The Archangel Michael is always presented at a certain angle; St. George is always holding his spear in a specified manner.

Master icon painters even worked from tracings of existing icons, the better to preserve these traditions. Artists rarely signed their icons, at least until the 18th century; icon painting was considered an act of piety rather than pride. Yet while there was little room for artistic expression, many icon painters have emerged as outstanding artists.

Prince Vladimir brought the first icon from Byzantium to Russia in the 11th century. This icon, the Virgin of Vladimir, still survives and is among the most revered in Russia. Russian icon painting soon set the standard for artists throughout the Orthodox world, growing in richness of expression until the art was abruptly halted with the Russian Revolution in 1917.

Icons generally were done with egg tempera on wood panels treated with gesso, a pastelike material applied to the painting surface. Earliest icons were done in mosaic tile; later, icons were embellished with pearls, semiprecious stones and baked enamel decoration. Gold leaf was widely used.

I rely on methods with which I am most

This icon and cross were collected in the Sitka area in the 1930s. (#9637-1, III-R, Alaska State Museum)

This icon of the Holy Mother and Christ Child was collected at Three Saints Bay in 1932. (#III R203, Alaska State Museum)

familiar: I work mostly with watercolor on D'Arches 100 percent rag. I use a variety of gold and metal leaf, some just 300-thousandths of an inch thick. Work must be done in an absolutely still room for the stuff really has a mind of its own and likes to float away at the slightest puff of air. The contents of our vacuum cleaner bags are the envy of the neighborhood.

The Russian Orthodox Church has a large number of saints who are presented as icons. Not the least of these are four Alaska saints canonized — or glorified, in the Church's terminology — for their contributions to the Spiritual Mission in Russian America. Alaska's four saints are Innocent, Herman, Juvenal and Petr the Aleut. Though icons existed of some of these saints, Innocent and Herman had been glorified as recently as 1977 and 1970 respectively; here was an opportunity to put some original thought and creative energy into a largely undeveloped subject.

I also have done a series of paintings of Russian Orthodox churches that form a significant part of the Alaska landscape. These churches are a vivid reminder of Alaska's Russian heritage.

A teacher by training, Byron Birdsall began painting in the late 1960s in Uganda, where he was teaching English through a U.S. government aid program. After traveling and painting in India, Hong Kong, Macau, American Samoa and New Zealand, Birdsall and his family settled in Anchorage in 1975. His art is displayed today in museums, homes and corporate offices throughout the United States. ■

Parishioners at St. Nicholas Russian Orthodox Church in Juneau celebrate, with the guidance of Father Jerome Cwiklinski, the Feast of the Epiphany which celebrates the baptism of Jesus by John the Baptist. (Al Grillo)

[Baranov's assistants] who took the cue from their chief. Efforts by the clergy to pursue their missionary duties and to resist Baranov's oppressive labor policies drew abuse and efforts at intimidation."

Setting off in July with an interpreter, Gideon began a tour of the entire island of Kodiak; after two months and five days, he reported performing 32 weddings and 503 baptisms, all but 22 of those for children. "I tried as best as I was able to instill into the newly enlightened what they needed for faith, some civic virtues and skills of husbandry," Gideon wrote of his visit to Alutiiq settlements. "To judge by external appearances, they seemed to listen to me willingly." He was welcomed with an array of traditional foods, from fish to berries mixed with whale fat. In exchange, Pierce writes, the monk made gifts of tobacco, cloth and sewing needles and goat's meat.

In 1805, Gideon reopened Kodiak's school, enrolling 50 students who pursued Russian grammar, arithmetic, geography and history. An Alutiiq speaker, the monk initiated work on a dictionary of Native languages and, Pierce says, organized an early attempt by Native students to compile an Alutiiq grammar. Invited by the unpredictable Nikolai Rezanov, a Russian American Co. founder, to submit a supply list for the mission, Gideon was specific: The monks needed provisions, tools and building material as well goods to be given to Natives as "payments and rewards," Pierce writes. "All of the above was refused with great indignation," Gideon noted.

In 1807, Gideon departed for Russia. After a stormy sailing, he eventually arrived at Petropavlovsk, traveling by sled dog in 1808 to inspect the Kamchatka region's eight churches and spending six years at Irkutsk before returning to St. Petersburg. Gideon's journals, detailing his voyage

from Kodiak of mistreatment of Natives. To learn more about conditions in America, where several of the first missionaries had joined mutinies against Baranov, priest-monk Gideon was sent as Orthodox Church envoy, arriving at Kodiak's St. Paul Harbor in July 1804. Gideon was to act as the church administration's eye in Kamchatka and Alaska. "Upon taking his post in Kodiak," writes historian Richard A. Pierce in *Russian America: A Biographical Dictionary* (1990), "Gideon was at once opposed by to Russian America and his time at Kodiak, are valued today by ethnographers and Orthodox Church historians alike, who published sections in 1894 to observe the Alaska mission's 100th anniversary.

Joy and Loneliness, Plenty and Want

Among Gideon's last tasks in Kodiak was to name as his successor Father German (anglicized Herman), among the original monks to arrive from Russia. The departing priest did not overlook the needs of Alaska Natives, praising Herman for a "kind and gentle attitude" that in turn fostered

BELOW: *Wildflowers and grass mark this Russian Orthodox gravesite on a hillside in the Unalaska cemetery. (Dan Parrett)*

RIGHT: *The Church of the Holy Ascension of Christ contains elements of the oldest Russian-built church still standing in the United States. It was designated a National Historic Landmark on April 15, 1970. (Cary Anderson)*

LEFT: *At Monk's Lagoon on Spruce Island, Father Martyrius of the St. Herman of Alaska Brotherhood stands in the intricately painted interior of the Meeting of the Lord Chapel, built by the monks in 1995. (Jim Lavrakas,* Anchorage Daily News*)*

ABOVE: *Fathers Martyrius, left, and Adrian share spiritual readings during mealtime. They subsist partially on food gathered from around Nelson Island, near Spruce Island, carrying on a tradition established by St. Herman. (Jim Lavrakas,* Anchorage Daily News*)*

"friendly relationships among [the Natives] and taught them to lead a more productive life."

Born near Moscow in a merchant-class town, Herman showed an early interest in good works and became a monk at 16, eventually transferring to the hard-working Valaam monastery where, Pierce notes, "with typical humility," he twice refused advancements, including a post with the Russian mission in Peking.

In Kodiak, Baranov's disdain for Herman's piety

and contemplative life on nearby Spruce Island was plain: "We have a hermit here now by the name of German, who is worse than [the priest-monk] Makarii [was]," grumbled Baranov in 1800, in a letter quoted by Pierce. "He is a great talker [and even though] he keeps himself to his cell most of the time, not even going to church out of fear of worldly temptations, nevertheless he knows everything that we think and do.... By means of pious cajoling, he extracts all the information he wants from pupils, the servants here and sometimes from our own men."

While he delighted in overhearing his brethren squabble mildly over Alaska turf (Juvenal and Makarii apparently were competitive), Herman was clear-eyed about the Alaska mission. His calling had brought him both "joy and loneliness," he wrote, "plenty and want, surfeit and famine, warm and cold."

Of all the original missionaries, Herman became famous and beloved, earning the name "Ap'a" (grandfather) among the Alutiiq. He started a school and orphanage, initiated the colony's first agricultural program and, perhaps to Baranov's dismay, advised high Russian officials. Among Orthodox faithful today, Father Herman is revered as a holy man and miracle-working prophet whose gravesite on Spruce Island attracts pilgrims seeking to drink from a spring the monk once blessed. Following his death in 1836, such were the stories of the beloved Herman that Bishop Veniaminov journeyed from Sitka to Kodiak in 1842 to learn more. But instead of the usual week, the wind-tossed sailing took 35 days; Veniaminov could not help noticing that only a half-cask of fresh water remained. "Towards evening our ship again approached Spruce Island," the bishop recalled in writings cited by Pierce. "I looked at the island and

said to myself, 'If, Father German, you have found the Lord's favor — let the wind change.'" Gusts soon relented and the schooner arrived safely that night.

In 1894, after veneration as a saint by local Natives, a chapel was erected over Herman's burial site; in 1970, the priest-monk was canonized in a two-day celebration on Kodiak Island. Today his reliquary within Kodiak's Holy Resurrection Church draws pilgrims from around the world, including some who report miraculous healings. His monastic residence at Monk's Lagoon is known as "New Valaam," in honor of Herman's Russian monastery.

Father Jerome Cwiklinski of Juneau blesses the Gastineau Channel during the Feast of the Epiphany celebration. (Al Grillo)

The Rev. Ioann Veniaminov:
Apostle to America

By Rosanne Pagano

EDITOR'S NOTE: *Between 1823 to 1837 while serving as a Russian Orthodox priest in Alaska, the Rev. Ioann (Ivan) Veniaminov regularly filed reports from the colony to his diocesan office in Irkutsk. The formal dispatches fill 12 journals and may be divided into two sections: arrival at Sitka in 1823 followed by 10 years of regional church duties in Unalaska, and relocation to Sitka in 1834 until his departure in 1849.*

Scholarly and compassionate, Veniaminov was well-suited to his times: Where other Russian authorities compelled the fealty of Native people, Veniaminov won their devotion by seeking first to understand. He crafted an alphabet for the Tlingit language and worked with Ivan Pan'kov, an Aleut chief, to devise an Aleut alphabet and a translation of St. Matthew's Gospel.

"We may read Aleut history as it was taking place," writes Alice Petrivelli in her foreword to the Journals of the Priest Ioann Veniaminov *(1993). "He knew our ancestors' gratitude and respect."*

Veniaminov's original journals are housed at the Alaska State Library at Juneau. Excerpts here are from Volume VII of the Rasmuson Library Historical Translation Series, University of Alaska Press.

The Rev. Ioann Veniaminov, canonized St. Innocent in 1979, sailed east for Sitka in 1823 from Okhotsk aboard the sloop Konstantin. The crossing, which followed a journey that had originated in Irkutsk some 1,200 miles to the southwest, took nearly two months: "I finally caught sight of Sitka," the cleric wrote in his journal, "and, after enduring a severe storm all night while sailing among many rocks, anchored safely at 8 p.m. on Oct. 20." He was 26, a promising seminarian, traveling with his mother, brother, wife and two young sons.

Despite the rigorous trip, Veniaminov appeared within two hours before Matvei Murav'ev, the colony's chief manager. The two met again on Oct. 23, when the priest announced his plans. "In order that I not live idly here for so long, I intended and desired to teach the students of the local schools as much as possible of God's law," Veniaminov stated in his journal. "I would teach the catechism at the school on Wednesday and Fridays from 9:00 to 11:00 and the readings at the church on Sunday, from 8:00 to 9:00, before the Liturgy."

On Oct. 24, Veniaminov's request for a translator — someone fluent in Russian and "Unalaskan" Aleut — was approved and Veniaminov's enduring legacy as an empathetic missionary and noted linguist began to take shape. "From this person, I could acquire in advance at least a few words of the language that I will need to know perfectly [to] address and edify the inhabitants of Unalaska," he wrote. A translator was found within three days.

Veniaminov was vigorous, flexible and pragmatic, traits rewarded still in rural Alaska where not all the comforts and regularities of home may be at hand. Where there was no chapel, the priest set up a tent and held services. Where there were

no schools, he opened them. After noticing one November Sunday that "not all" of his students managed to arrive on time for the 9 a.m. service, but did begin to gather near the end, the priest won approval from Murav'ev to teach the Gospel lesson on Mondays, when pupils were assembled at school. "The change," Veniaminov noted, "results from the fact that at nine o'clock, it is still dark and it is cold in the church."

While the first Russian Orthodox baptism in the Unalaska area was recorded in 1762 and the Spiritual Mission arrived at Kodiak in 1794, official missionary work in Alaska slowed for about 20 years, ending in the 1820s. Veniaminov, the first resident priest assigned to the sprawling parish, did not arrive until 1824; by 1867, church records show, there were some 15,000 faithful in the colony anchored by St. Michael's Cathedral in Sitka, as well as nine churches, 35 chapels, nine priests and two deacons.

As detailed in the journals, Veniaminov's work was ceaseless. He led church services — daily during Lent — and performed baptisms, marriages and funeral services. He heard confessions, recited traditional prayer services for sea travelers and traveled by baidarka to give Final Communion to the sick. A typical journal entry reads: "We set out at 5 o'clock. At 2:30 we arrived at the village of Pavlovskoe on the Alaska Peninsula. After Vespers and Matins, I instructed the young people. I invited all of the adults into a iurt and then read to them from my sermon. After that I heard Confession from 35 of the local inhabitants."

Traveling in 1824 through the stormy Aleutians, sometimes leading his party through snow by foot, Veniaminov was moved by the reception of villagers who decades later remembered him as "the good father."

"It is impossible to remain silent about the zeal, devotion and affectionate manner of all the local Aleuts," Veniaminov notes in the journals. "They have only to catch sight of the baidara and all — from the small to the great, and even those on crutches — come to greet us, and to receive the blessing with great joy. They see us off in the same manner." By December 1825, construction of Unalaska's Church of the Holy Ascension of Christ, designed by Veniaminov himself, was well under way.

"All the doors have been built, as have been the entire lower story, all the windows and the ceiling in the sanctuary," a journal entry states. "The entire church is roofed." Veniaminov is said to have finished the iconostas, a carved wooden screen painted with icons, himself.

He was an early chronicler of Native life. Published in 1840, "Notes on the Islands of the Unalashka District," is among Veniaminov's great works; his Aleut grammar, published in 1846 and consulted for a century, was awarded a prize by the Russian Academy of Sciences. Accurate translations of the Russian Orthodox catechism, the Gospel of St. Matthew and his own sermon, "A Brief Indication of the

Born Ioann (Ivan) Evseevich Popov on Aug. 26, 1797, at Anga, a village along the Angara River near Irkutsk, the son of the sacristan at the local church would rise 70 years later to rule all of Russian Orthodoxy as Metropolitan of Moscow. The name Veniaminov was assigned to him in 1814 when the bishop of Irkutsk, Veniamin, died and church officials wanted the name perpetuated because they admired the bishop. Artist Nicolai Kolupaiev captures Veniaminov's stateliness in this painting of the clergyman at Sitka. (Ernest Manewal)

Way to the Heavenly Kingdom," occupied the priest. "I checked these texts strictly, correcting them for grammar," Veniaminov noted on April 29, 1837. "Now, I dare say that these translations are as correct and as clear and flawless as possible, given the present state of the Aleut language."

A weather observer whose instruments were supplied by the Academy of Sciences, Veniaminov, who had never been south of 52 degrees N in his life, indulged in a bit of awe on first experiencing the benign Northern California climate during a visit to Fort Ross in 1836. "I must admit," he wrote, "that the healthful air, the pure blue sky, the geographical position and the native vegetation all immediately strike and captivate, (especially) one who has lived on Unalaska and Sitka."

In 1840, after learning that his wife had died in Irkutsk a year earlier, Veniaminov took monastic vows (his children would be

supported by the church and emperor); in a St. Petersburg ceremony that year, Veniaminov was named Bishop Innocent with authority over Kamchatka and the Kurile and Aleutian islands. As bishop, Veniaminov agreed to the arrival in 1840 of the first Lutheran pastor in Alaska in response to requests from Finns settled in New Archangel.

Veniaminov returned to Alaska in 1841 to establish a Sitka seminary and extend missionary work to the Kenai, Yukon River and Nushagak regions. In 1843, he consecrated the chapel at Sitka's Russian mission, a two-story building today known as the Bishop's House; in 1849 Sitka's Church of the Holy Trinity was dedicated with the goal of serving Tlingit Indians.

Elevated as archbishop in 1850 and assigned to the city of Blagoveschensk, 950 miles east of Irkutsk, Veniaminov oversaw a diocese that took in the Amur River region; much of the next 10 years was spent touring his far-flung district. In 1868, the priest who held church services in makeshift tents was elevated as Metropolitan of Moscow, the church's highest administrative post. The revered cleric known for his dedication to education, the poor and missionary work died in 1879. He was buried in a chapel at Sergeyev Posad northeast of Moscow, and canonized nearly a century later with the designation "apostle to America."

"If personal humility is greatness," one observer wrote in a 1947 edition of The British Columbia Historical Quarterly, "then Veniaminov may be truly named one of the church's greatest men." ■

EDITOR'S NOTE: *A former associate editor of ALASKA GEOGRAPHIC®, Rosanne Pagano is now an associate professor at the University of Alaska Anchorage.*

Martyrs and Saints

The priest-monk Juvenal, among Herman's brethren, traveled to mainland Alaska in 1795 and baptized large numbers of Natives from Prince William Sound to the Kenai Peninsula. In 1796, he moved still farther inland, beyond present-day Iliamna Lake, and made his way northwest toward the Bering Sea. Encountering a Yupik

hunting party near Quinhagak, both the priest and his Athabaskan guide were slain, apparently at the order of the local shaman. Veniaminov relates that the priest was killed by Natives; Bishop Gregory Afonsky, writing in *A History of the Orthodox Church in Alaska*, (1977), says the attack may have stemmed from Juvenal's attempt to remove some children from the newly baptized to be schooled in Kodiak.

Still other accounts suggest the priest may have been the victim of cultural misunderstanding when the local shaman mistook Juvenaly's brass pectoral cross for the metal chains worn by intruding Siberian counterparts. Today Juvenal is revered as a martyred saint, canonized in Alaska in 1980.

Misconceptions of his death stem in part from a "diary" attributed to Juvenal and detailing misconduct that historians erroneously concluded had provoked the killing. Cited by Bancroft, the writings took on a life of their own until Bancroft's own interpreter acknowledged fabrications. Archbishop Afonsky says that after researching Russian sources, he was unable to find any trace of the Juvenal diary. Scholars seeking to understand Alaska's rich Russian past keep the "diary" in mind when trying to discern truth from formal documents and uncertain accounts alike.

Questions also surround the death in Spanish California of Chungangnaq, known as Petr the Aleut, who became the first Orthodox Christian martyr in the New World.

Metropolitan Theodosius (left), head of the Russian Orthodox Church in America until 1973, and Patriarch Aleksy II, Patriarch of Moscow and all Russia, the spiritual leader of the Russian Orthodox Church, emerge from St. Innocent Orthodox Christian Cathedral in Anchorage. (Al Grillo)

Russian Orthodox and Athabaskan styles merge in the Theotokos Prayer Chapel in Eklutna Historical Park north of Anchorage. (Loren Taft/Alaskan Images)

Traveling in 1815 with Russian hunters seeking to poach sea otters off the California coast, Petr apparently was among 24 Aleuts seized by Spanish authorities. Pierce states that 15 of the prisoners were delivered to Russian authorities in 1817; others would be produced later, the Spanish said, or allowed to stay if they had married and accepted Catholicism.

In 1819, the crew of a Russian brig arrived at one of the Santa Barbara Channel Islands in southern California and rescued an Aleut prisoner, Ivan Keglii, who was taken to Fort Ross. Under questioning there, Pierce says, Keglii claimed to have been among the prisoners taken in 1815; Spanish priests had tried to convert him and Chungangnaq. When both men refused, Keglii said a priest ordered Chungangnaq's torture: The Aleut's fingers and arms were severed and finally he was killed by disemboweling.

While Herman, Veniaminov and Russian American Co. historian P.A. Tikhmenev all found the report credible, contemporary authorities including Pierce note that Keglii's account is unconfirmed and seems uncharacteristic of the Spanish missionaries. When word of Petr's death reached Herman in Kodiak, the priest is said to have crossed himself, declaring, "Holy new martyr Petr, pray to God for us." Petr was canonized in 1980 with Juvenal.

Living Testimony in a New Land

While *promyshlenniki* amassed pelts and Russian American Co. investors banked their dividends, the Spiritual Mission's success in Alaska was harder to quantify. As Anchorage historian Barbara Sweetland Smith points out, Orthodox monks were financially dependent on the company until it quit the colony and were supported thereafter by the imperial treasury. What then did Russia get for its spiritual investment in Alaska?

In a letter in 1805 following a visit to the colony,

The reconstructed Russian blockhouse and grave of Iakov Netsvetov, the first Creole priest, stand atop a hill in Sitka. (Ernest Manewal)

Rezanov, a top-ranking Russian American Co. official, complained about the monks, whom he considered underworked and meddlesome: "[They] have baptized several thousands here, but only nominally," Rezanov declared in a letter cited by Pierce. While the Spiritual Mission laid early groundwork in Alaska, the church's legacy may be traced to 1824, when Ivan (Ioann) Veniaminov was dispatched to the colony, becoming the first resident priest in Unalaska before transferring at the company's request to the capital at Sitka in 1834.

In 1840, Veniaminov became bishop of Kamchatka and the Kurile and Aleutian islands; in 1868 he was elevated to Metropolitan, head of the Imperial Russian church. "In every position he held," Smith notes, Veniaminov's work was "characterized by an attention to literacy, education and development of local, that is Native, leadership of the mission."

Here, then, was Orthodoxy's benchmark of success, borrowed in part from the Russian American Co.'s own policy of developing local talent: "The Creole clergy were in effect living testimony of the church's work in the new land," writes historian Antoinette Shalkop in *Russia's American Colony* (1987). Just four years after Veniaminov's arrival, Alaska had produced its first Creole priest, Iakov Netsvetov, born in 1804, the son of a Russian American Co. employee.

Raised on St. George Island, Netsvetov entered the Irkutsk seminary, married a Russian woman in 1826 and was ordained a priest in 1828. He served in storm-tossed Atka, as the village's first resident priest. Netsvetov oversaw the building of a school that offered a "regular" curriculum, Pierce states, and a subsistence life for students who relied on their own summer gardens as well as company aid.

Like his mentor and lifelong friend Veniaminov, Netsvetov's mind was nimble, his interests varied and his writings voluminous. Netsvetov hunted, translated the Gospels into Aleut and prepared marine-life specimens for Russian museums. Like Veniaminov, Netsvetov was tolerant; both men were well-regarded by authorities and their congregations.

In 1842, two years after taking monastic vows as Innokentii and becoming bishop of Alaska, Veniaminov visited Netsvetov in Atka and the two traveled on to Kamchatka. Pierce observes that the bishop probably prevailed on Netsvetov during this journey to accept a transfer to the Alaska mainland. (Netsvetov's own request to enter monastic life at Irkutsk had been approved in 1839 but was conditioned on locating a replacement in Atka; none was found.) Veniaminov's plan apparently was to dispatch Netsvetov to Kenai and name another priest to the new mission at St. Michael Redoubt on the Bering Sea coast. When the Russian American Co. pointed out that the Yukon mission should be self-sufficient, Veniaminov selected the widowed and childless Netsvetov.

In 1845, Netsvetov took up his new assignment, a lone priest in the wilderness. He learned Yupik, erected a new church and painted its icons, all to win another outpost for Orthodoxy. After seven years in "this severe and cold climate," Netsvetov sought a transfer: "My illnesses and attacks have increased so much that now I find myself unable to serve in this part of the country," he told Veniaminov.

But the bishop, assuring his Yukon priest that God would send helpers, declined to act. In 1853, Netsvetov journeyed up the Yukon to the Innoko River where he preached to hundreds, relying on Creole guides and translators. "Imagine my joy," the priest wrote in his daily record, "seeing so many people, former enemies, united in Christ."

In all, Netsvetov would spend nearly 20 years at

the Yukon mission, eventually losing his health and eyesight and enduring reprimands for overspending despite explanations that safe travel required a contingent of hired Native men. In 1863, Netsvetov was relieved and went to Sitka where his wife, Anna, had died in 1836. The priest himself died in 1864 and was buried near the door of the Tlingit Church of Sitka; it is no longer standing. Canonized in Anchorage in 1990, Alaska's first Creole priest is remembered today as the "enlightener and baptizer" of Native peoples. ∎

A Russian-American scholar, author and college instructor, the Rev. Michael J. Oleksa received his doctoral degree from the Orthodox Theological Faculty of Czechoslovakia. He is an archpriest at St. Innocent Russian Orthodox Cathedral in Anchorage.

Sts. Sergius and Herman Russian Orthodox Church lights up a winter night in Nanwalek (English Bay) on the Kenai Peninsula. Father Herman (German), one of the original missionaries, was considered by many to be a fair and compassionate priest. In 1970, he was canonized as the first American saint of the Orthodox Church, and St. Herman's Orthodox Theological Seminary in Kodiak is named for him. (Al Grillo)

The Alaska Purchase

By Rosanne Pagano

A Matter of Public Business

The handwritten note arriving at the home of U.S. Sen. Charles Sumner one March night in 1867 was urgent and brief: "Can you come to my house this evening?" wrote Secretary of State William H. Seward. "I have a matter of public business in regard to which it is desirable that I should confer with you at once."

So began Sumner's introduction to a U.S.-Russian deal that would culminate, less than two weeks later, in the Senate's approval by a 37-2 vote of a treaty leading to the Alaska Purchase. Sumner, a lawyer, former Harvard lecturer and Massachusetts Republican, chaired the Senate's Foreign Relations Committee but he had been unaware until Seward's message that an Alaska treaty was close. In fact, the Russian Ministry of Foreign Affairs had raised the possibility of a sale as early as 1857, following Russia's defeat in the Crimean War. While the ministry wisely urged that any overtures to the United States be confidential to avoid undercutting the Russian American Co., word leaked anyway; it

would be another decade, in which the Alaska question was overshadowed by the U.S. Civil War and political stirrings that in 1868 led to an impeachment resolution against President Andrew Johnson, before Treasury Warrant No. 9759 was issued and Alaska became a U.S. territory.

Exactly why Russia sold and the United States bought has occupied historians on both sides of the Bering Strait ever since. "The colony was more of a strategic than an economic liability," states historian James R. Gibson. As Russia eyed the North American advances of England, its enemy, a sale of Russian America to anyone but the British became appealing. "In case of war, this colony will be at the mercy of every hostile power," wrote diplomat Eduard Stoeckl, representing Russia in the treaty talks. With the discovery of gold in the Northwest, Russia anticipated its colony could be overrun by

FACING PAGE: *The Alaska, U.S., and Russian American Co. flags fly together at Castle Hill in Sitka as a reminder of a shared history. (Harry M. Walker)*

stampeders. Even in peacetime, Stoeckl noted, Alaska's distance from Russia made it prey for "American freebooters" already crowding the Pacific.

Examining his country's motives to sell in light of 19th century Russian American relations, Moscow-based historian N.N. Bolkhovitinov outlines a convergence of factors, ranging from

The $7.2-million United States treasury draft that paid for the purchase of Alaska is dated more than one year after the Treaty of Purchase was signed due to the political climate and the House of Representatives' investigation into the disposition of the money. (National Archives, Washington, D.C.)

Russia's desire to concentrate attention on its Far East and Amur River holdings, to the scant Russian population in Alaska, numbering fewer than 800. Bolkhovitinov also notes the "difficult but not critical" health of the Russian American Co.; the risk of troubled relations with Alaska Natives; and political reforms that had whittled at the serf system on which the colony depended.

Based on his study of a pivotal meeting in 1866, attended by Alexander II, foreign minister Aleksandr Gorchakov, Konstantin (the emperor's brother), and Stoeckl, among others, Bolkhovitinov concludes that by selling Alaska, Alexander hoped to shed a potential political "hotbed," forge a sustaining alliance with the United States, and strengthen Russia's Far East position. Noteworthy

too is a statement by Catherine II outlining as early as 1788 what Russia did not want from its colony: "The examples of American settlements are not flattering," she observed. "A great dispersion into the Pacific will not be beneficial." Political and social momentum — and to a lesser degree historical will — helped propel Russia's inclination to sell.

Seward's interest in Alaska is easier to trace: A devoted expansionist, his career includes efforts to add the Hawaiian Islands as well as two islands in the Danish West Indies to the United States. Seward also entertained the Dominican Republic's inquiries to join the union. He was not, however, the single-minded caricature portrayed in political cartoons: Seward's anti-slavery beliefs, for instance, kept him from endorsing a U.S. purchase of Cuba.

Trained as a lawyer, Seward was a prominent critic of slavery and in 1849 joined the Senate. After failing to win the Republican presidential nomination in 1860, he campaigned for Abraham Lincoln and joined his cabinet as secretary of state. On the night Lincoln was killed, Seward was attacked as well, at his home, by a knife-wielding conspirator of John Wilkes Booth; Seward recovered and served as secretary of state under Johnson until 1869.

Seward desired Alaska's annexation because it fit into his long-standing view of the nation's place on the continent, the hemisphere and the globe. In this respect, strategic mutual ground could be found with the emperor, who had concluded that his country's best interest argued for sale. The rest was up to Congress, a body so hostile to Seward and Johnson that Stoeckl once remarked he was relieved the treaty had not immediately faced a Foreign Relations Committee vote, as Seward wanted; Stoeckl believed the proposal would have been promptly defeated to rebuke the secretary of state.

Prince Dmitrii Maksutov was the last governor of Russian America, 1865-67. (#PCA 01-3397, Alaska State Library)

North Pacific Shores Are Swarming

Seward, who did not visit the territory until 1869, apparently never felt the pangs of buyer's remorse. But Sumner, who became the treaty's Senate linchpin, could not help wonder initially if the millions to be appropriated for Alaska should go instead to the South, where post-Civil War reconstruction was under way. "Which is better?" he mused, "to spend money for South to help Union, or for this?"

Sumner was soon to replace his unmodified "this" with an exhaustive knowledge of Alaska encompassing its climate, furs, fisheries and minerals as well as population, geography and its potential value to the United States. While Seward's foes caterwauled — lampooning Russian America as "Walrussia" or, as the solidly anti-Seward *New York Tribune* called it, "a territory of ice, snow and rock" — Sumner began a crash course on Alaska.

As historian Margaret Shannon notes in *Russian*

America: The Forgotten Frontier, Sumner's briefing was initiated by noted naturalist Spencer F. Baird. An assistant secretary at the Smithsonian Institution, Baird offered the senator a chance to interview Smithsonian colleagues who'd spent time at Sitka and Norton Sound.

He tantalized with what was known and unknown about the territory: "The shores of the Pacific are swarming with animals of economical importance — cod, salmon, fur seals — [while] the islands abound in coal," said Baird. He noted that while much information had been amassed by the telegraph expedition of 1865-67, much work such as mapping Alaska's interior remained to be done. "I hope the purchase of Russian America as proposed will be authorized by the Senate," Baird said, promptly arranging to meet with Sumner, an expansionist with his own hopes of acquiring Canada.

A special legislative session, meeting in closed session, began April 1, 1867. Lawmakers had been scheduled to adjourn March 30, a Saturday, but were waylaid by an unexpected message from Johnson, read by the clerk: "I transmit to the Senate, for its consideration with a view to ratification, a treaty between the United States and His

FACING PAGE: This painting by Emmanuel Leutze of the Alaska Treaty of Purchase signing shows the intense discussion between key players William H. Seward (seated to the left of the globe), Russian minister to Washington Eduard Stoeckl (standing with his hand on the globe), and Sen. Charles Sumner (seated next to Stoeckl). (#VA142, Alaska State Museum)

RIGHT: William Henry Seward, secretary of state during the administrations of Presidents Lincoln and Johnson, was instrumental in persuading the U.S. government to buy Alaska from Russia. Though the transaction was reduced to nicknames such as "Seward's folly" and "Seward's icebox," historians know now the value of his enthusiasm. (#VA 145, Alaska State Museum)

Majesty, the Emperor of all the Russias...." The deal, signed that day by both countries, called for Russia to cede its colony to the United States. Washington insiders sitting down to dinner that night could talk nothing else.

A magnetic observatory, installed as a means of determining changes in the earth's magnetism through time, was maintained by Russian American geologists on Japonski Island (at center), a stone's throw from downtown Sitka. The information their studies supplied helped the U.S. Coast and Geodetic Survey start a base of geologic data on Alaska. (File photo)

Following 4-2 approval in Sumner's Foreign Relations Committee (where two opponents quipped their votes would change if Seward was forced to move to Alaska), the treaty moved to the full Senate. On April 8, Sumner rose to speak, building his comments out of brief notes: "Important to consider character of country. But — treaty will be ratified with references to other considerations. Advantages to the Pacific coast." By his own estimate, Sumner's address filled two hours, 45 minutes. The treaty was ratified a day later by the deceptively lopsided vote of 37-2.

While Sumner's exact words are lost because no

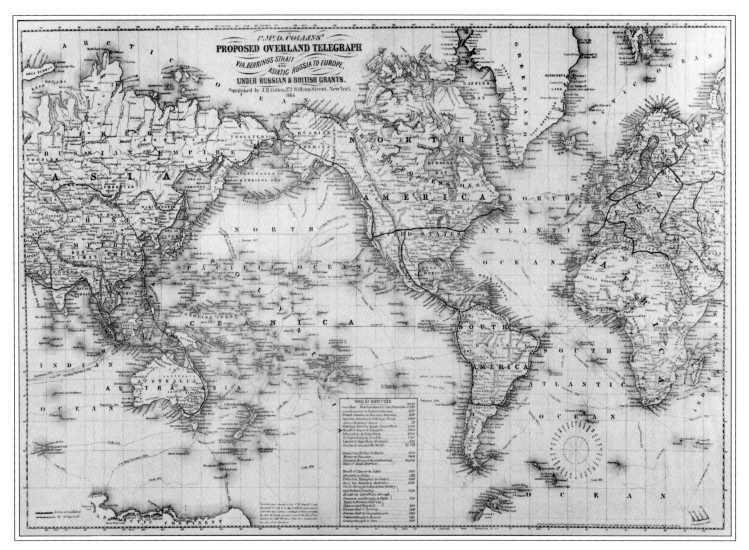

P. MᶜD. COLLINS'
PROPOSED OVERLAND TELEGRAPH
VIA BEHRINGS STRAIT
AND
ASIATIC RUSSIA TO EUROPE,
UNDER RUSSIAN & BRITISH GRANTS.
Furnished by J.H.Colton,172 William Street, New York.
1864

records were kept of the closed-door session, his thoughts live on in a written version of the speech, published May 24, 1867. Writing to his friend Henry Wadsworth Longfellow, Sumner acknowledged that his decision to support the treaty had had "a decisive influence;" he felt a responsibility to capture his speech on paper. The senator knew

Scientists who accompanied the U.S. Signal Service on its work in Alaska as part of the Western Union (Collins Overland) Telegraph Expedition of 1865-67 provided much of the basic information that helped Congress decide to buy Alaska from Russia. (#1864 G3201, Alaska and Polar Regions Archives, Rasmuson Library, University of Alaska Fairbanks)

Possession Plates

By Steve Henrikson

Like their European and American counterparts, Russian explorers left durable monuments of their North American travels. The Russians placed wooden crosses, iron plates and double-headed eagle crests, among other items, along exploration routes during the late 18th and early 19th centuries — years of intense international competition for the valuable resources of the Northwest Coast and Alaska.

The Russians buried possession plates in North America as far south as California. This one is a cast of a pewter plate now in the San Diego Historical Society Collection. (Alaska State Museum)

Jealous of their competitors' intentions in Alaska, Russians solidified their claims by placing fixed and portable markers. Many markers once delineated Russian claims in Alaska, but only a few survive today. In total, these objects communicated a firm message: No vacancy.

The most visible markers could be seen from offshore. Crosses placed on prominent headlands marked imperial claims as well as the spiritual domain of the Russian Orthodox Church. Cross Mountain above Sitka is named for a Russian cross once planted at the summit.

Other markers were known only to those who placed them. Metal plates and other objects buried in secret offered indisputable proof of possession should Russian claims be contested.

Alaska Natives were incorporated into Russia's efforts to mark and claim new "discoveries." Silver and gold medals, exhibiting the bust of Empress Catherine II, the double-headed eagle, or the words "Allies of Russia" were bestowed upon Native leaders. Natives regarded the medals as tokens of deserved respect and often gave gifts in return.

To the Russians, these tokens were a means of bolstering the status of cooperative leaders who engaged in peaceable trade. The presents advanced Russia's geopolitical goals by warning rival nations that Natives were subjects of the Russian crown.

In addition to medals, Natives were given portraits of the Russian emperor, fancy military-style jackets and written documents. Natives were instructed to wear or display their gifts prominently when American "Boston Men" and English "King George's Men" came calling.

Bronze sculptures of the double-headed eagle, symbol of Russian imperial authority, were the most elaborate ornaments given to Natives. Measuring 9-1/2 inches tall, these crests were presented on poles, decorated with feathers and ribbons, or offered as breastplates. Only two of these crests survive today. One example, now in the Alaska State Museum in Juneau, was presented to the Kiks.ádi clan of the Sitka Tlingit as a peace offering following Russia's seizure of land for its headquarters at Sitka in 1804.

Another crest was excavated in 1934 from a Klickitat Indian grave on an island in the Columbia River, and is now in the Smithsonian Institution. Found approximately 150 miles up the river from the coast, it probably was traded from a coastal tribe in contact with Russian seafarers.

Ironically, while Alaska was being claimed for Russia, some Alaska Natives put in a claim of their own. Upon sighting the first seaborne explorers, the Taantakwaan Tlingit of Tongass Village claimed 'The First White Man" as a crest. Among the Tlingit of Southeast Alaska, important historical events and experiences inspire the adoption of a crest — a distinctive symbol unique to the lineage — that may be represented by totemic artwork. Eventually, the Taantakwaan commissioned a totem pole to display this crest, and President Abraham Lincoln (whose image apparently was deemed representative of his race) served as a model. The Lincoln figure from this pole is preserved in the Alaska State Museum.

Medals and other gifts presented to Natives were useful but easily destroyed, stolen or replaced by rival traders; they could not serve as the only means of marking new Russian territories. To leave a more permanent sign, Russian explorers buried at least 20 metal plates along the Pacific Coast. In 1787, Ivan Iakobi, governor general of Irkutsk, ordered Russian traders to "affirm the acquisition of all the newly acquired part of America [by] marking the land with signs appropriate and natural to the might and name of Russia."

The following year, the first of these plates were planted by navigators Gerasim Izmailov and Dmitrii Bocharov. They set sail carrying five numbered plates, each marked with a cross and the words "Russian Territory." As the men cruised through Prince William Sound, Yakutat Bay and Lituya Bay, they buried the plates and carefully mapped the sites.

The entire operation was considered a state secret. Burial locations were kept from the crew and from Native people who prized all metals for tool making.

All the efforts at secrecy were canceled — and the burial locations revealed — when the Izmailov and Bocharov travel journals were stolen and published without permission. In 1802, Aleksandr Baranov was ordered to move the original plates as quickly as possible and to stealthily plant more. Russians continued burying metal plates until at least 1811 although there are no accounts of unearthings to prove Russian ownership. Following the sale of Alaska to the United States in 1867, the plates remained buried and forgotten.

In the mid-1930s, the Civilian Conservation Corps began an excavation of Russia's first settlement at Sitka, St. Archangel Michael's Redoubt (or Old Sitka,

Russian possession plaque #12, found in 1936 at Old Sitka, the first Russian fort in southeast Alaska, was made of thin sheet copper. It is now part of the collection of the Sitka National Historical Park. (Alaska State Museum)

approximately six miles north of the current city). At a depth of 24 inches, sandwiched between four large bricks, excavators uncovered a heavily-corroded iron plate bearing Cyrillic letters: Country in Possession of Russia, No. 12.

According to Russian documents, this plate was issued to Aleksandr Baranov in 1790 and probably buried on his first reconnaissance of the Sitka area in 1795. The only numbered example known to exist today, the plate is part of the Sitka National Historical Park collection.

An unlettered pewter tablet bearing the double-headed eagle crest was unearthed in southern California in 1960 in the backyard of a Coronado Island resident. The style of the double-headed eagle may be of 1850s vintage though references to unnumbered crests are found in Russian documents dated much earlier. The San Diego Historical Society owns a casting of this plate but the location of the original is unknown.

In recent years, several systematic attempts have been made to locate more buried markers. Historians Richard A. Pierce and Alexander Doll searched in 1971 for markers left by Izmailov and Bocharov, using original maps and written descriptions of sites. Another expedition led by Russian navigator and historian Leonid Lysenko of Vladivostok searched in 1993 for a plate believed to have been buried near Nanwalek, near the tip of the Kenai Peninsula.

That both attempts were unsuccessful should not be surprising — but not for lack of effort or sound scholarship. Even if the vague clues from Russian archives could lead archaeologists to the sites, 200 years or more have come and gone since the plates were buried; construction or natural forces likely have disturbed the ground and landscape. Too, corrosion may have reduced the metal plates to rusty stains in the soil.

Twentieth-century explorers had at least one tradition in common with Russians who once sailed Alaska's coast: Plaques were placed on the moon by Apollo crews and sent into deep space mounted on probes. In Alaska, Russia's territorial markers today are enduring symbols of a nation's expansionist dreams. ◻

Writer Steve Henrikson is collections curator at the Alaska State Museum in Juneau.

that while public opinion after the vote generally supported purchase, Alaska still tended to conjure images of barren expanse and forlorn landscapes.

Sumner wrote: "I have been tried a good deal by the Russian Treaty, which has given us a new world with white foxes and walruses not to be numbered. At last I made up my mind that I could not take ground against it."

Breeder of Trouble

Seward's interest in Russian America dated to at least 1846 when he foresaw a time when U.S. borders would reach "the icy barriers of the North." As biographer John M. Taylor notes, Seward referred to the expansion again in 1860 while on the campaign trail for Lincoln; during the Civil War, as the Confederate raider Shenandoah burned American whaling ships in the Bering Sea, Seward became convinced that a U.S. Navy presence in the region was needed. He may also have wanted Russian America for the United States to keep another power from infringing on the continent.

Except for Washington Territory's fishermen, who eyed Alaska's abundant waters, no organized lobby pressed for the purchase. Lack of a constituency mattered little to Seward, who preferred the expediency of negotiating out of the public eye. When Stoeckl returned to Washington from St.

Petersburg after convincing the foreign ministry that Russia's colony was a "breeder of trouble" and it was time to sell, Stoeckl turned to Seward, with whom he had dealt throughout the Civil War. A meeting of the two men in March 1867 was called to consider U.S. fishermen's requests for trading rights; when Stoeckl made it clear the emperor was not interested, "Seward asked whether he might consider selling his North American possession outright," Taylor says, adding that "Stoeckl was encouraging but noncommittal."

A veteran diplomat married to an American and living in Washington since 1856, Stoeckl was well-positioned to broker the treaty. But even if the Russian aristocrat had grown used to America's dreams of manifest destiny, the speed with which Seward consummated the deal was unexpected. After his meeting with Stoeckl in March, Seward won authority from Johnson to enter into purchase talks. Stoeckl's approved minimum was $5 million; when Seward offered that sum, the Russian countered with a demand for $10 million. Seward suggested $7 million and another $200,000 to satisfy any Russian American Co. claims; with the compromise, a tentative agreement was at hand.

As his son and biographer Frederick Seward recalled, the secretary of state was home at his whist table on March 29 when Stoeckl arrived to announce that the emperor had cabled approval;

Sen. Charles Sumner, in his defense of the Alaska Purchase before the Senate on April 8, 1867, included lists of Alaska's natural abundance. His assumptions turned out to be true. This 1908 photo reveals thousands of salmon caught in traps in Funter Bay on Admiralty Island in Southeast Alaska. (#PCA 311-14, from Canneries and Mining in Southeast Alaska Collection, Alaska State Library)

a treaty could be signed the next day. "Why wait till tomorrow? Let us make the treaty tonight," replied Seward, who may have wished to prevent a bidding war if England entered the picture.

Stoeckl pointed out that his secretaries were not at their desks, Seward's own clerks were absent and the secretary of state's office was closed for the night. Frederick Seward writes that his father, who had received the emperor's news with "a smile of satisfaction," was undeterred: "If you can muster your legation together before midnight," Seward told Stoeckl, "you will find me awaiting you at the department, which will be open and ready for business." While Congress slumbered, the $7.2 million treaty was translated and signed; by 4 a.m. on March 30, the papers were dry.

Initially undecided about the purchase, Sumner

apparently had understood that an Alaska purchase should focus debate on the nation's future, not Seward's ambitions; in a move that would buy needed time, the senator declined Seward's request that the treaty be immediately approved.

"Cash paid for cast-off property," read a satirical ad in Horace Greeley's *New York Herald,* which also ran an editorial: "Mr. Seward's dinner table is

spread regularly with roast treaty, boiled treaty, treaty in bottles ... treaty clad in furs, ornamented with walrus teeth, fringed with forest and flopping with fish."

A scoffing press was the public price Seward paid for cinching the treaty literally under cover of dark. But, as Taylor notes, stakes were far higher in Congress, where Seward's decision to sign first and find allies later could have derailed his work — and his dream — altogether. "Seward ran a risk that the Senate might balk at being handed a monumental land transaction by an administration that had few supporters on Capitol Hill," Taylor observes.

The Origin of the Scheme

After relaying word of Russian ratification on May 15, Stoeckl began to envision his "adieu" to Washington as soon as 1868. But even while Russian and U.S. troops gathered for the formal

transfer in Sitka on Oct. 18, 1867, Congress had yet to agree on payment. "Seward assured Stoeckl that the money would be voted as soon as Congress convened in December, but he may have had doubts," writes Taylor. A little more than a month after Russia's double eagle flag was lowered for the last time in Alaska, the House resolved in a 93-43 vote to no longer underwrite Seward's manifest destiny desires; in November, the House unanimously approved a motion asking the Judiciary Committee to see if Congress was bound to pay under the treaty or had "the right to grant or refuse, at its discretion." By spring of 1868, news accounts poking fun at the deal — Alaska cows were said to give ice cream, not milk — gave way to a whiff of scandal.

A news story published as early as April 1, 1868, suggested there may be a congressional investigation "to ascertain the origin of the scheme and

Charles Sumner Champions the Alaska Purchase

EDITOR'S NOTE: *An encyclopedic speech delivered behind closed doors April 8, 1867, by Sen. Charles Sumner is widely credited with swaying votes in favor of Alaska's purchase. Sumner began by addressing undecided colleagues, acknowledging that the treaty seemed to pose a stark political choice — historic expansion into vast, resource-filled lands, or a legacy of millions of dollars squandered on ice.*

As Eduard Stoeckl saw it, initial negative reaction from Sumner's Foreign Relations Committee was just anti-Seward politics: "Several senators said to me that they had nothing against the transaction itself," wrote Stoeckl, "but that they could not confirm an act which bore the signature of Mr. Seward."

On April 9, one day after Sumner's address and a mere 10 days after he first learned of the proposal, the Alaska Purchase treaty passed the Foreign Relation's Committee 37-2. The senators, Stoeckl confided in a dispatch home, "were converted one by one."

A nationally prominent Republican from Massachusetts, Sumner asked that his remarks be made public; after his revisions, the two-hour-plus speech expanded to fill a 48-page pamphlet published a month after the committee vote. Edited and excerpted here, the speech is an enduring compendium of Alaska's wonders and eccentricities.

Climate is the key to this whole region.... Heat and cold, rain and fog, to say nothing of snow and ice, which play such a part in this region, are not abnormal but according to law known only of late years.... [He then explains the Pacific's thermal current and its influence on Alaska weather.]

[Capt. James] Cook records that in his opinion, 'cattle might exist in Ounalaska [Unalaska] all the year round without being housed' and this was in latitude 53 [degrees] 52', on the same parallel with Labrador and several degrees north of Quebec; [yet] the climate of Quebec does not continue across the continent... [the] Pacific coast of our continent is warmer than the corresponding Atlantic coast. The flora on the American side, even in the Bering Strait, is more vigorous than that on the Asiatic side; the American mountains have less snow than their Asiatic neighbors....

The forests at Sitka are so wet that they will not burn, although frequent attempts have been made to set them on fire. In 1828, there were 20 days when it rained or snowed continuously; 120 when it rained or snowed part of the day and only 66 days of clear weather. The island of Kodiak and the recess of Cook Inlet are outside this climatic curve, so as to be comparatively dry....

On Norton Sound, winter may be said to commence at the end of September, although the weather is not severe till the end of October. The River Yukon is navigable for at least four, if not five, months in the year. The snow packs hard at an average of 2-1/2 feet deep. The ice is 4 or 5 feet thick; in a severe winter it is 6 feet thick. Life at Fort Yukon under these rigors of nature, although not inviting, is not intolerable.

Berries in Profusion

Cook finds in Prince William Sound "Canada and spruce pine, some of them tolerably large." [French explorer] Jean La Perouse [describes] pines measuring 6 feet in diameter and 141 feet in height....

Turning westward from Cook Inlet the forests on the sea line are rarer until they entirely disappear. But where trees are wanting, grass seems to abound. This is the case with Kodiak, the peninsula of Alaska and the Aleutian Islands generally. On the Bering Sea, the forests do not approach the coast except at the heads of bays and sounds, although they abound in the Interior and extend even within a short distance of the Frozen [Arctic] Ocean....

But even in the northern latitudes, the American coast is not without vegetation. Grass here takes the place of trees.... Next after trees, early navigators speak oftenest of berries, which they find in profusion [and] next to berries were plants for food and these were in constant abundance. Bering, on landing at the Shumagin Islands, observed the Natives 'to eat roots which they dug out of the ground, and scarce shaked off the earth before they eat them....' La Perouse, who landed in latitude 58 degrees, 37', finds a French bill of fare, including celery, chicory, sorrel and 'almost all that exists in the meadows and mountains of France....

Since the establishment of Europeans on this coast, an attempt has been made to introduce nutritious grains and vegetables known to the civilized world but without very brilliant success. Against wheat and rye and against orchard fruits there are obstacles of climate perhaps insuperable....

[Sumner notes that cattle failed to thrive in Sitka, where there was too much rain and too little pasture.] Hogs are more easily sustained but feeding on fish instead of vegetable products, their flesh acquires a fishy taste which does not recommend it. Nor has there been greater success with poultry, for this becomes prey of the crow, whose voracity here is absolutely fabulous....

The Bones of Elephants

Beginning at the south we have Sitka and its associate islands, composed chiefly of volcanic rocks, with limestone near. Little is known of the coast between Sitka and Mount St. Elias which, itself a volcano, is the beginning of a volcanic region occupying the peninsula of Alaska and the Aleutian Islands, and having no less than 30 volcanoes, some extinct but others still active. North of Alaska and near the mouth of the Kwichpak [Yukon River], the coast seems to be volcanic or metamorphic, and probably tertiary, with a vein of lignite near the head of Norton's Sound. At the head of Kotzebue Sound, the cliffs abound in the bones of elephants and other extinct mammals, together with those of the musk ox and animals now living in the same latitude. From Kotzebue Sound northward, the coast has a volcanic character....

It is not entirely certain that iron has been found in this region, although frequently reported. At 66 degrees, 35' Kotzebue found a false return in his calculations, which he attributed to the disturbing influence of 'iron.'

Silver also has been reported at Sitka [and], like the iron, in 'sufficient quantity to pay for the working.'

Copper is to be found on the banks of the Copper River [in] masses sometimes as large as 40 pounds. Of this there can be little doubt. Traces of copper are also found in other places on the coast; also in the mountains near the Yukon where the

Indians use it for arrow heads.

Coal seems to exist all along the coast; traces of it are reported on the islands of the Sitkan archipelago, and this is extremely probable for it has been worked successfully on Vancouver Island below. It is also found on the Kenaian [Kenai] Peninsula, Alaska [Peninsula], the island of Unga, Ounalaska, and far to the north at Beaufort [and] it is supposed that there are extensive beds in the neighborhood better in quality....

Gold is less important than coal but its discovery produces more excitement. [Here Sumner cites surveys done by Russian geologist Petr Doroshin from 1847 to 1852.] He reports gold in at least three different localities, each of considerable extent. The first is the mountain range north of Cook Inlet and extending into Alaska. About the same time, certain Indians from the Bay of Yakutat, not far from Mount St. Elias, brought him specimens of diorite found in their neighborhood. [In] the summer of 1855, [Doroshin] found gold on the southern side of Cook Inlet, in the mountains of the Kenai Peninsula.... Thus much for the mineral resources of this new-found country as they have been recognized at a few points on the extensive coast, leaving the vast unknown Interior without a word.

Animals of the Chase

A Russian officer who was one of the early visitors to this coast remarks that the only prospect of relief for the suffering Natives 'consists in the total extirpation of the animals of the chase,' which he thought from the daily havoc must take place in a very few years....

From 1797 to 1817, [the] Ounalaska district yielded upwards of 2.5 million seal skins and from 1817 to 1838, the same

district yielded 579,000 skins. Assuming what is improbable, that these skins were sold at 25 rubles each, some calculating genius has ciphered out the sum total of proceeds at more than 85 million rubles, or, calling the ruble 75 cents, a sum total of more than $63 million. Clearly the latter years can show no approximation of any such doubtful result....

From a competent source I learn that the value of skin at Sitka during the last year

Although initially lukewarm on the subject at best, Sen. Charles Sumner of Massachusetts became a staunch advocate of U.S. purchase of Alaska. His support brought the Senate around to a vote of 37-2 in favor of the treaty. (Library of Congress)

Near Kodiak, he reports that 'having three hours calm [weather], his people caught upward of a hundred halibut, some of which weighed 100 pounds and none less than 20 pounds.' [Stopping] at Ounalaska, he reports 'plenty of fish, at first mostly salmon [and] once a halibut that weighed 254 pounds....'

Officers of the U.S. Navy report the same fish substantially which Cook reported as far north as the Frozen Ocean. Scientific explorers, prompted by the Smithsonian Institution, report cod in Bering Strait, on the limits of the Arctic Circle....

Salmon exist in unequaled numbers, so that this fish, so aristocratic elsewhere, becomes common enough; [its] capture is the daily reward of the humblest.... Herring seem not to be less multitudinous than the salmon. Their name, derived from the German heer, signifying an army, is amply verified. [Sumner concludes this section by noting that abundance is not enough; for an Alaska industry to prosper, suitable fishing grounds, weather and markets all must be considered.]

Mr. President, I now conclude my examination. [As] these extensive possessions, constituting a corner of the continent, pass from the imperial government of Russia they will naturally receive a new name. How shall they be called? ...

Following these Natives whose places are now ours, we too should call this 'great land' Alaska. ■

was substantially as follows: sea otter, $50; marten, $4; beaver, $2.50; bear, $4.50; black fox, $50; silver fox, $40; cross fox, $25; red fox, $2....

By and by the [fur] commerce was engrossed by the Russians and the English. And now it passes into the hands of the United States, with all the other prerogatives belonging to this territory.

A Dainty Little Fish

Nothing is clearer than that fish in great abundance are taken everywhere on the coast, around the islands, in the bays and through the adjacent seas. Here are oysters, clams, crabs and a dainty little fish of the herring tribe called the oolachan [hooligan], contributing to the luxury of the table, and so rich in its oily nature that the Natives are said to use it sometimes as a 'candle.'

Besides these [are] those great staples of commerce and mainstays of daily subsistence, salmon, herring, halibut, cod, and behind all the whale. Here is the best the sea affords for the poor or the rich; for daily use or for the fast days of the church. Here also is a sure support at least to the inhabitants of the coast.

At Nootka Sound, [Cook] reports fish 'more plentiful than birds,' of which the principal sorts in great numbers were 'the common herring, scarcely exceeding seven inches in length, and a smaller sort, the same with the anchovy or the sardine,' and now and then 'a small brownish cod, spotted with white.'

what is behind it. Nobody believes that the whole $7 million will go into Russian coffers." Historian Paul S. Holbo notes that while newspapers soon pursued the issue, "neither Seward nor his allies bothered to respond to these vague charges of corruption." In March, the House struck again, this time postponing consideration of the Alaska payment for two months — a stall tactic that violated the treaty's provision of payment within 10 months of ratification.

"Seward swung into action, demonstrating that he had not entirely lost his powers of persuasion," Taylor writes. Following a House vote on July 14, 1868, gold began to move from Washington to St. Petersburg. Among Seward's allies in the House battle were U.S. Rep. Thaddeus Stevens, chairman of the House Appropriations Committee and a leader of the Johnson impeachment effort, and U.S. Rep. Nathaniel Banks, chairman of the House Committee on Foreign Relations. Winning Stevens to the cause helped distinguish treaty issues from the impeachment, Taylor notes, while Banks was advised of Alaska's natural resources wealth.

But scandal rumors persisted and on Dec. 19, 1868, Seward was called to testify before the House Committee on Public Expenditures. "Congressional inquiries then were primitive but often as harried and tendentious as in recent times," writes Holbo in *Tarnished Expansion: The Alaska Scandal, the Press and Congress, 1867-1871* (1983). "[The] results of the inquiry embarrassed accusers and accused like, and unwittingly tarnished expansion."

Soldiers in Sitka fire an Independence Day salute three years after the Alaska Purchase. Alaska was under U.S. Army jurisdiction until it officially became a Territory in 1912. (Alaska State Library)

A Generation to Appreciate

The House hoped to learn exactly how much, if any, of the $7.2 million payment had failed to reach Russia. One Massachusetts-based newspaper, *The Spy,* reported as much as $2 million was missing; anonymous government officials as well as lobbyist Robert J. Walker, Banks and Seward himself were alleged to have collected large amounts.

Committee testimony had uncovered a discrepancy between the amount shipped and the amount received, but sums appeared to be far less than news accounts had suggested. While the full amount had been received by Stoeckl, he had forwarded $7,035,000 — "the balance was credited to his own account," Taylor writes. Out of the balance went $26,000 to Walker, who testified to the sum, and $4,000 to editor-lobbyist John W. Forney.

"There is no doubt," concludes Holbo, that "the Russian minister disbursed some of the moneys at

his disposal to Walker, [lawyer Frederick P.] Stanton, [lobbyist Robert W.] Latham, Forney and other newspapermen." Holbo notes that Stoeckl may also have garnered a "larger portion" for himself. "He had been sorely disappointed by what he considered the emperor's meager compensation for his outstanding services in negotiating the treaty.... He would never be called to account in the United States."

In his House testimony, Seward acknowledged a role in circulating Sumner's speech and a pro-treaty article by Walker. He rejected any notion that favorable press reports had been purchased by his office, and he insisted he knew nothing of how Stoeckl may have disbursed the payment. "I know of no payment to anybody, by him, or any application of the funds which he received."

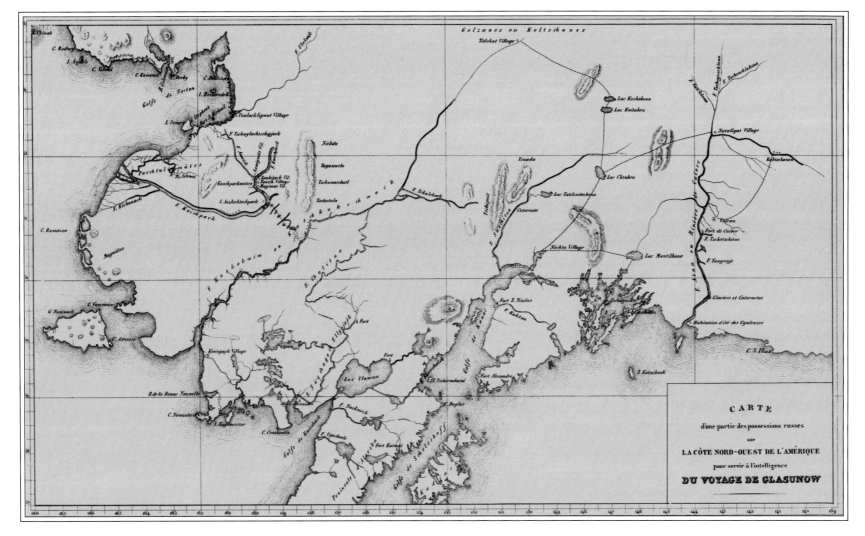

CARTE

d'une partie des possessions russes

sur

LA CÔTE NORD-OUEST DE L'AMÉRIQUE

pour servir à l'intelligence

DU VOYAGE DE GLASUNOW

A handwritten memo by Johnson may shed more light. As Taylor recounts, the president and secretary of state chatted during a carriage ride to Maryland about the Alaska appropriation in September 1868, two months after funds had been approved. "The Secretary asked [if] it had ever occurred to me how few members there were in Congress whose actions were entirely above and beyond pecuniary influence."

The memo, which quotes Seward but does not suggest his sources, claims that while House consideration of the payment dragged on, Forney had been paid $30,000; Walker and Stanton received $20,000; Banks $8,000; and Stevens $10,000. "All these sums were paid by the Russian minister directly and indirectly to the respective parties to secure appropriation of [the treaty] money," Johnson wrote. (Other sources suggest that Seward also claimed Stevens' share to be only $1,000, a sum that went undelivered when Stevens died.)

On Feb. 27, 1869, the committee's inconclusive report appeared. While critical of press accounts of alleged vote buying, the committee conceded it lacked information from Russian officials who could not be compelled to appear. "The investigation was *ex parte* in an undesired sense, and consequently barren of affirmative or satisfactory negative results." For newspapermen who had made careers reporting on the Alaska Purchase, the intrigue — and thus the interest — had begun to slip away. "Congress busied itself with adjournment and much of the press momentarily turned elsewhere," notes Holbo.

Looking back on his career, Seward once declared the Alaska purchase to be his finest work but predicted "it will take the country a generation to appreciate it." Experts do not quibble with his assessment. Proving himself astute through Johnson's impeachment, humane in denouncing slavery and forward-thinking in his interest in China and the Suez and Panama canals, Seward managed to navigate the politics of his day by envisioning the future. ■

The Legacy of Russian America

By Barbara Sweetland Smith

Russia sold Alaska to the United States in 1867 and scores of Russian nationals sailed away from Sitka, the old capital of Russian America. The influence of those Russians, however, is still a prominent feature of Alaska at the end of the 20th century, and makes Alaska unique within the fabric of North American history. This legacy is both evident and hidden. The legacy may be experienced firsthand by visiting one of the scores of Orthodox churches which thrive in Alaska communities from Atka in the Aleutian Islands to Russian Mission on the Yukon River and from Bethel to Sitka. It may be heard in the Slavic names of cities, rivers, mountains, inlets, straits and bays. The influence of those Russian colonists of long ago may be heard also wherever Aleut, Alutiiq and Yupik are spoken. Less visible to the casual observer is the heritage of biological naming and describing that enriches our knowledge of Alaska and the North.

The Orthodox Church embodies several features of the rich and manifold Russian legacy. First there is the religion itself, Eastern Orthodoxy, which is the faith of a majority of Alaska's Native community, including almost all Aleuts and Alutiiqs, as well as sizable followings among the Yupik, Tlingit and Athabaskans. Russian laymen administered the first Christian baptisms in Alaska as early as 1759, on Umnak Island in the Aleutian Chain. From that time, the Orthodox faith has made a deep impression on the Native Alaskan community and it remains strong throughout the former Russian America. In 1972, 18 Orthodox clergy served in Alaska. By the end of this century, the number had grown to 33, ministering in some 80 towns and villages; 25 of them Alaska Native, many of these trained at St. Herman's Theological Seminary in Kodiak. This school was founded in 1973 to train indigenous clergy to meet the needs of a burgeoning

FACING PAGE: *The New Archangel Dancers perform at Sitka to honor the community's Russian roots. Although performances are held throughout the year, the dancers and other Sitkans remember their Russian heritage with special celebrations each October on Alaska Day. (Ernest Manewal)*

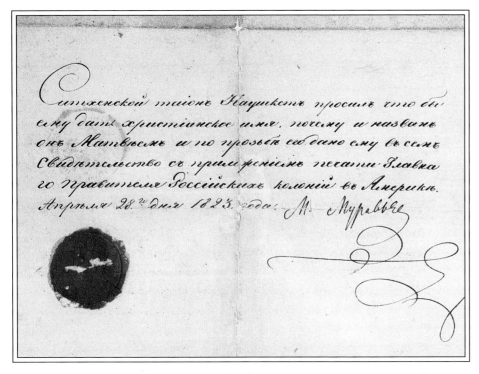

Russia would not take root in North America. The dean of Alaska's historians, Hubert Howe Bancroft, in 1886 declared unequivocally: "...the Greek [sic] Church was a failure throughout Russian America.... It is nowhere recorded, except by the priests themselves, that...the teaching of the ecclesiastics made much impression on the natives." History, indeed, has proven Bancroft to be very wide of the mark. The Orthodox faith has not only failed to fade away, but it has grown, being even more widespread today than in 1867, particularly in the Yukon-Kuskokwim region.

The Church and its clergy also met a number of important needs which built a reservoir of affection and loyalty among Alaska Natives. Priests served throughout the Russian period and later even in the American era as a buffer between the excesses of government and the local people. The church also was a haven of learning, a place where a talented Aleut, Alutiiq or Tlingit youngster could attend school and move forward into a successful career within the Russian colonial administration. Because of the scarcity of Russians in the colony, there was opportunity for local people. A number of Creoles served in every capacity from teacher to shipwright, priest to naval officer. One Aleut, Alexander Kashevarov, retired in Russia as a major general. There was no racial discrimination in the Russian service.

Orthodox revival. The canonization in 1970 of North America's first Orthodox saint — a missionary to Alaska — stimulated this revival. Bishops and Archbishops from all over the world converged on Kodiak to recognize the sanctity of the monk Herman, who had come as a missionary in 1794. Within the next 20 years, Orthodoxy would elevate two more saints and two martyrs from the Alaska missionary era.

The enduring popularity of a Russian institution among Alaska Natives may seem puzzling. Indeed, for many decades after Russia sold Alaska, it was assumed that the Russians had left only a bad memory, and certainly no lasting cultural legacy. Although Christianity had also outlasted Spanish colonialism in America, many historians and public figures assumed that Eastern Christianity from

One of the most important elements of the Russian legacy is the survival of Native languages. This is particularly significant when one considers the zeal with which American officials attempted to destroy the use of indigenous speech after 1884, and sadly, until recent times. Professor Michael Krause of the University of Alaska's Center for Alaska Native Languages has gone so far as to say that whatever else one may say about colonial rule, the Russians "did only good for the heritage of our Native languages." They accomplished this through an active program to develop literacy throughout Russian America, first by documenting Native languages, then by creating alphabets and dictionaries and finally by translating sacred texts and sermons into Native languages. In addition, within the church itself, the liturgy was conducted in the local language. Even during the period of language repression in the American era, the prohibition against using Native languages did not reach into the Church and it was there that the oral tradition survived.

A legacy also resides in wood and paint. Thirty-six churches and several secular buildings from the era of Russian America are on the National Register of Historic Places. Thirteen Russian sites, including five churches, are National Historic Landmarks. Public policy and private philanthropy in recent years have supported the preservation of these historic structures, with technical support and funds. The Aleut community itself has organized a non-profit society to raise funds for

the conservation of its liturgical treasures. The World Monuments Fund in 1997 declared the Church of the Holy Ascension of Christ at Unalaska to be one of the most important endangered historic sites in the world.

Besides the people themselves, many of whom carry the names of Russian forebears or godfathers,

Bearing a name recognized throughout Alaska, Aleksandr Maslov-Bering, a direct descendant of Vitus Bering, stands with a replica of the explorer's ship, the St. Peter, at Unalaska in 1991. (Douglas Veltre)

and the historic structures from the Russian era, Russia's legacy is no less important in the area of science. Naturalists traveled on many of the Russian ships during the 120 years of colonial rule. They were prodigious recorders, documenting Native languages and culture, as well as flora, fauna, rocks and minerals. A few of the scientists are well known. Georg Steller's name is familiar to many. He is identified with the Steller's jay and the endangered Steller sea lion. His most important work, however, lies in documenting creatures which are now extinct: the northern or Steller sea cow (*Hydrodamalis gigas*) and the spectacled cormorant (*Phalocrocorax perspicillatus*). Both of these natives of the Commander Islands in the Bering Sea proved too tasty for their own good and were brought to extinction by Russian fur hunters within less than a hundred years after their discovery. Without Steller's meticulous records of the sea cow, nothing would be known of this behemoth of the north. But Steller was only the first of a long line of distinguished naturalists who did important work in Alaska. The most significant of these is Adelbert von Chamisso. Chamisso was a poet and a botanist, a German of French birth who traveled with the Kotzebue expedition of 1815, and who made prodigious collections of and reports on plants in the Aleutians, in the Bering Straits area and also in San Francisco Bay. Chamisso also is responsible for the first published studies of North Pacific whales. The documentation and collections that resulted from these voyages provide invaluable information about early Alaska. For many years, it was hard to access this resource because of the ice curtain between Russia and America. Now, much of this knowledge is coming to light through an "open door" policy at Russian museums and archives.

Closely related to this passion for collecting the natural world was the Russian zeal to collect evidence of the material culture of Native Americans. Russian museums contain the oldest collections from many parts of Alaska and northern California and have much to tell about life at the dawn of western contact. Russia's visual artists, traveling as scientific recorders on voyages of exploration and supply, also produced hundreds of images that reveal ritual and ordinary life, tools and boats, clothing and housing. The collections and the artistic legacy provide unique insights for Alaskans into their distant heritage.

The Russian era in Alaska came to an official end in 1867, but the legacy grows even more apparent as we continue to study Russian America, discovering new facets to this intriguing epoch. The richly articulated services of a primarily Native Alaskan Orthodox church, the dignity of historic structures, the survival of written and oral Native languages, and the scientific and cultural record accumulated by perceptive travelers on the Russian ships all remind us that it is Russian America that makes Alaska unique among the 50 United States. ■

A leading authority on Russian America, Barbara Sweetland Smith has been curator of several exhibits on this subject at the Anchorage Museum of History and Art including: Russian America, The Forgotten Frontier (1990-92); Heaven on Earth, Orthodox Treasures of Siberia and North America (1994-97); and the forthcoming Science Under Sail, Russia's Great Voyages to America, 1741-1867, opening in 2000. In addition, she was project director for the Aleut Church Restitution Project for the Aleutian-Pribilof Islands Association, and author of A Sure Foundation, Aleut Churches in World War II *(1994). This effort lead to ongoing federal grants totaling $4 million for restoration of Aleut churches damaged during World War II.*

Bibliography

Afonsky, Bishop Gregory. *A History of the Orthodox Church in Alaska (1794-1917)*. Kodiak: St. Herman's Theological Seminary, 1977.

Barnett, Anthony W. and Schumacher, Paul J.F. *An Analysis of the Archaeological Excavation by the U.S. Forest Service at Old Sitka, Alaska, in 1934-1935*. Manuscript, Sitka National Historical Park, National Park Service, 1967.

Barratt, Glynn. *Russia in Pacific Waters, 1715-1825*. Vancouver: University of British Columbia Press, 1981.

Bolkhovitinov, Nikolai. "The Sale of Alaska in the Context of Russian American Relations in the Nineteenth Century," pp. 156-71, vol. 2, no. 2, November 1990, *Pacifica: A Journal of Pacific and Asian Studies*. Edited by Robert D. Craig. Anchorage: Pacific Rim Studies Center, Alaska Pacific University in cooperation with the Cook Inlet Historical Society, 1990.

Boraas, Alan. *Report of a Portion of the Admiral Nevelskoi Russian Expedition to Southcentral Alaska 1993*. Manuscript, Kenai Peninsula College, Soldotna, 1993.

Divin, Vasilii A. *The Great Russian Navigator, A.I. Chirikov*. The Rasmuson Library Historical Translation Series, vol. 6, translated and annotated by Raymond H. Fisher, series editor Marvin W. Falk. Fairbanks: University of Alaska Press, 1993.

Foster, Mary, and Henrikson, Steve. *Symbols of Russian America: Imperial Crests and Possession Plates in North America*. Concepts, technical paper no. 5. Juneau: Division of Libraries, Archives, and Museums, Alaska State Department of Education, 1995.

Gibson, James R. "Bostonians and Muscovites on the Northwest Coast, 1788-1841," pp. 81-119. *The Western Shore: Oregon country essays honoring the American Revolution*. Edited by Thomas Vaughan. Portland: Oregon Historical Society [1975?].

—. *Imperial Russia in Frontier America: The Changing Geography of Supply of Russian America, 1784-1867*. Cartographer, Miklos Pinther. New York: Oxford University Press, 1976.

—. *Otter Skins, Boston Ships, and China Goods: The Maritime Fur Trade of the Northwest Coast, 1785-1841*. Seattle: University of Washington Press, 1992.

Henning, Robert A.; Morgan, Lael; Olds, Barbara; and Phillips, Carol A., eds. *The Aleutians*, vol. 7, no. 3. Anchorage: Alaska Geographic Society, 1980.

Holbo, Paul S. *Tarnished Expansion: The Alaska Scandal, the Press, and Congress 1867-1871*. Knoxville: The University of Tennessee Press, 1983.

Howay, Frederic William. *A List of Trading Vessels in the Maritime Fur Trade, 1785-1825*. Edited by Richard A. Pierce. Kingston, Ontario: The Limestone Press, 1973.

Khlebnikov, Kirill T. *Baranov: Chief Manager of the Russian Colonies in America*. Translated by Colin Bearne, edited by Richard A. Pierce. Kingston, Ontario: The Limestone Press, 1973.

Kisslinger, Jerome, trans. *Journals of the Priest Ioann Veniaminov in Alaska, 1823 to 1836*. The Rasmuson Library Historical Translation Series, vol. 7, introduction and commentary by S. A. Mousalimas, series editor Marvin W. Falk. Fairbanks: University of Alaska Press, 1993.

Kraus, David H., translator. *Russian Exploration in Southwest Alaska: The Travel Journals of Petr Korsakovskiy (1818) and Ivan Ya. Vasilev (1829)*. Fairbanks: University of Alaska Press, 1988.

Middleton, John. *Clothing in Colonial Russian America: A New Look*. Kingston, Ontario: The Limestone Press, 1996.

Miller, David H. *The Alaska Treaty*. Kingston, Ontario: The Limestone Press, 1981.

Morgan, Lael, ed. *Alaska's Native People,* vol. 6, no. 3. Anchorage: Alaska Geographic Society, 1979.

Murray, John. *Alaska*. Oakland: Fodor's Travel Publications, 1997.

Nordlander, David J. *For God and Tsar: A Brief History of Russian America 1741-1867*. Anchorage: Alaska Natural History Association, 1998.

Okun, Semen B. *The Russian-American Company*. Translated by Carl Ginsburg. Cambridge: Harvard University Press, 1951. (Reprinted 1979, Octagon Books, New York.)

Orth, Donald J. *Dictionary of Alaska Place Names*. Washington, D.C.: U.S. Government Printing Office, 1967.

Pierce, Richard A. *Russian America: A Biographical Dictionary*. Kingston, Ontario: The Limestone Press, 1990.

— and Doll, Alexander. "Alaskan Treasure," *The Alaska Journal*, vol. 1, no. 1, pp. 2-7. Juneau: Alaska Northwest Publishing Co., 1971.

— and Donnelly, Alton S., eds. *A History of the Russian American Company*, vol. 2: *Documents*. Translated by Dmitrii Krenov. Kingston, Ontario: The Limestone Press, 1979.

—, ed. *Russia in North America: Proceedings of the 2nd International Conference on Russian America, Sitka, Alaska, August 19-22, 1987*. Kingston, Ontario: The The Limestone Press, 1990.

—, ed. *Notes on Russian America, Part I: Novo-Arkhangel'sk*. Compiled, with introduction and commentaries, by Svetlana G. Fedorova, translated by Serge LeComte and Richard A. Pierce. Kingston, Ontario: The Limestone Press, 1994.

—, ed. *Notes on Russian America, Parts II-V: Kad'iak, Unalashka, Atkha, the Pribylovs*. Compiled, with introduction and commentaries, by R. G. Liapunova and S. G. Fedorova, translated by Marina Ramsay. Kingston, Ontario: The Limestone Press, 1994.

Rennick, Penny, and Campbell, L.J. *Sitka*. Alaska Geographic Guides series, Anchorage: Alaska Geographic Society, 1995.

—, ed. *Kodiak*, vol. 19, no. 3. Anchorage: Alaska Geographic Society, 1992.

—, ed. *Unalaska/Dutch Harbor*, vol. 18, no. 4. Anchorage: Alaska Geographic Society, 1991.

Russian American Company 1802, 1817-67: Records of the Russian-American Company, Correspondence of the Governors General. Microfilmed by National Archives, Washington, D.C.

Index

Shelikhov, Gigorii I. "A Voyage to America, 1783-1786." Edited and translated by Richard A. Pierce. *Alaska History*, No. 19. Kingston, Ontario: The Limestone Press, 1981.

Shiels, Archie W. *Seward's Icebox: A Few Notes on the Development of Alaska, 1867-1932.* Bellingham, 1933.

Shur, Leonid. *The Khlebnikov Archive: Unpublished Journal (1800-1837) and Travel Notes (1820, 1822, and 1824).* The Rasmuson Library Historical Translation Series, vol. 5, translated by John Bisk, editor Marvin W. Falk. University of Alaska Press, 1990.

Smith, Barbara S. *Russian Orthodoxy in Alaska: A History, Inventory, and Analysis of the Church Archives in Alaska.* Published for the Alaska Historical Commission, 1980.
— and Barnett, Redmond J., eds. *Russian America: The Forgotten Frontier.* Tacoma: Washington State Historical Society, 1990.
—; Goa, David J.; Bell, Dennis G. *Heaven On Earth: Orthodox Treasures of Siberia and North America.* Anchorage Museum of History and Art, 1994.

Starr, S. Frederick, ed. *Russia's American Colony.* Durham: Duke University Press, 1987.

Taylor, John M. *William Henry Seward: Lincoln's Right Hand.* New York: HarperCollins, 1991.

Tikhmenev, Petr A. *A History of the Russian-American Company.* Translated and edited by Richard A. Pierce and Alton S. Donnelly. Seattle: University of Washington Press, 1978.

VanStone, James W. "Russian Exploration in Interior Alaska: An Extract from the Journal of Andrei Glazunov," *Pacific Northwest Quarterly* 50(2), pp. 37-47. 1959.
—, ed. "V. S. Khromchenko's Coastal Explorations in Southwestern Alaska, 1822," Translated by David H. Kraus. Fieldiana: *Anthropology* 64. Chicago: Field Museum of Natural History, 1973.

Wright, Miranda Hildebrand. *A Thesis: The Last Great Indian War (Nulato 1851).* Fairbanks, 1995.

Zagoskin, Lavrentii A. *Lieutenant Zagoskin's Travels in Russian America, 1842-1844.* Translated by Penelope Rainey, edited by Henry N. Michael. Toronto: University of Toronto Press, 1967. ■

STATEMENT OF OWNERSHIP, MANAGEMENT AND CIRCULATION

ALASKA GEOGRAPHIC® is a quarterly publication, home office at P.O. Box 93370, Anchorage, AK 99509. Editor is Penny Rennick. Publisher and owner is The Alaska Geographic Society, a non-profit Alaska organization, P.O. Box 93370, Anchorage AK 99509. *ALASKA GEOGRAPHIC®* has a membership of 4,240.

Total number of copies 9,360

Paid and/or requested circulation
    Sales through dealers, etc. 0
    Mail subscription 4,240
Total paid and/or requested circulation 4,240
Free distribution 100
Total distribution 4,340
Copies not distributed (office use, returns, etc.) 5,020

Total 9,360

I certify that the statement above is correct and complete.

—Kathy Doogan, Co-Chair, Alaska Geographic Society

ALASKA GEOGRAPHIC. Back Issues

The North Slope, Vol. 1, No. 1. Out of print.
One Man's Wilderness, Vol. 1, No. 2. Out of print.
Admiralty...Island in Contention, Vol. 1, No. 3. $19.95.
Fisheries of the North Pacific, Vol. 1, No. 4. Out of print.
Alaska-Yukon Wild Flowers, Vol. 2, No. 1. Out of print.
Richard Harrington's Yukon, Vol. 2, No. 2. Out of print.
Prince William Sound, Vol. 2, No. 3. Out of print.
Yakutat: The Turbulent Crescent, Vol. 2, No. 4. Out of print.
Glacier Bay: Old Ice, New Land, Vol. 3, No. 1. Out of print.
The Land: Eye of the Storm, Vol. 3, No. 2. Out of print.
Richard Harrington's Antarctic, Vol. 3, No. 3. $19.95.
The Silver Years, Vol. 3, No. 4. $19.95.
Alaska's Volcanoes, Vol. 4, No. 1. Out of print.
The Brooks Range, Vol. 4, No. 2. Out of print.
Kodiak: Island of Change, Vol. 4, No. 3. Out of print.
Wilderness Proposals, Vol. 4, No. 4. Out of print.
Cook Inlet Country, Vol. 5, No. 1. Out of print.
Southeast: Alaska's Panhandle, Vol. 5, No. 2. Out of print.
Bristol Bay Basin, Vol. 5, No. 3. Out of print.
Alaska Whales and Whaling, Vol. 5, No. 4. $19.95.
Yukon-Kuskokwim Delta, Vol. 6, No. 1. Out of print.
Aurora Borealis, Vol. 6, No. 2. $19.95.
Alaska's Native People, Vol. 6, No. 3. Limited.
The Stikine River, Vol. 6, No. 4. $19.95.
Alaska's Great Interior, Vol. 7, No. 1. $19.95.
Photographic Geography of Alaska, Vol. 7, No. 2. Limited.
The Aleutians, Vol. 7, No. 3. Out of print.
Klondike Lost, Vol. 7, No. 4. Out of print.
Wrangell-Saint Elias, Vol. 8, No. 1. Limited.
Alaska Mammals, Vol. 8, No. 2. Out of print.
The Kotzebue Basin, Vol. 8, No. 3. Out of print.
Alaska National Interest Lands, Vol. 8, No. 4. $19.95.
Alaska's Glaciers, Vol. 9, No. 1. Revised 1993. $19.95.
Sitka and Its Ocean/Island World, Vol. 9, No. 2. Out of print.
Islands of the Seals: The Pribilofs, Vol. 9, No. 3. $19.95.
Alaska's Oil/Gas & Minerals Industry, Vol. 9, No. 4. $19.95.
Adventure Roads North, Vol. 10, No. 1. $19.95.
Anchorage and the Cook Inlet Basin, Vol. 10, No. 2. $19.95.
Alaska's Salmon Fisheries, Vol. 10, No. 3. $19.95.
Up the Koyukuk, Vol. 10, No. 4. $19.95.
Nome: City of the Golden Beaches, Vol. 11, No. 1. $19.95.
Alaska's Farms and Gardens, Vol. 11, No. 2. $19.95.
Chilkat River Valley, Vol. 11, No. 3. $19.95.

Alaska Steam, Vol. 11, No. 4. $19.95.
Northwest Territories, Vol. 12, No. 1. $19.95.
Alaska's Forest Resources, Vol. 12, No. 2. $19.95.
Alaska Native Arts and Crafts, Vol. 12, No. 3. $24.95.
Our Arctic Year, Vol. 12, No. 4. $19.95.
Where Mountains Meet the Sea, Vol. 13, No. 1. $19.95.
Backcountry Alaska, Vol. 13, No. 2. $19.95.
British Columbia's Coast, Vol. 13, No. 3. $19.95.
Lake Clark/Lake Iliamna, Vol. 13, No. 4. Out of print.
Dogs of the North, Vol. 14, No. 1. $21.95.
South/Southeast Alaska, Vol. 14, No. 2. Limited.
Alaska's Seward Peninsula, Vol. 14, No. 3. $19.95.
The Upper Yukon Basin, Vol. 14, No. 4. $19.95.
Glacier Bay: Icy Wilderness, Vol. 15, No. 1. Limited.
Dawson City, Vol. 15, No. 2. $19.95.
Denali, Vol. 15, No. 3. $19.95.
The Kuskokwim River, Vol. 15, No. 4. $19.95.
Katmai Country, Vol. 16, No. 1. $19.95.
North Slope Now, Vol. 16, No. 2. $19.95.
The Tanana Basin, Vol. 16, No. 3. $19.95.
The Copper Trail, Vol. 16, No. 4. $19.95.
The Nushagak Basin, Vol. 17, No. 1. $19.95.
Juneau, Vol. 17, No. 2. Limited.
The Middle Yukon River, Vol. 17, No. 3. $19.95.
The Lower Yukon River, Vol. 17, No. 4. $19.95.
Alaska's Weather, Vol. 18, No. 1. $19.95.
Alaska's Volcanoes, Vol. 18, No. 2. $19.95.
Admiralty Island: Fortress of Bears, Vol. 18, No. 3. $21.95.
Unalaska/Dutch Harbor, Vol. 18, No. 4. $19.95.
Skagway: A Legacy of Gold, Vol. 19, No. 1. $19.95.
Alaska: The Great Land, Vol. 19, No. 2. $19.95.
Kodiak, Vol. 19, No. 3. Out of print.
Alaska's Railroads, Vol. 19, No. 4. $19.95.
Prince William Sound, Vol. 20, No. 1. $19.95.
Southeast Alaska, Vol. 20, No. 2. $19.95.
Arctic National Wildlife Refuge, Vol. 20, No. 3. $19.95.
Alaska's Bears, Vol. 20, No. 4. $19.95.
The Alaska Peninsula, Vol. 21, No. 1. $19.95.
The Kenai Peninsula, Vol. 21, No. 2. $19.95.
People of Alaska, Vol. 21, No. 3. $19.95.
Prehistoric Alaska, Vol. 21, No. 4. $19.95.
Fairbanks, Vol. 22, No. 1. $19.95.
The Aleutian Islands, Vol. 22, No. 2. $19.95.

Rich Earth: Alaska's Mineral Industry, Vol. 22, No. 3. $19.95.
World War II in Alaska, Vol. 22, No. 4. $19.95.
Anchorage, Vol. 23, No. 1. $21.95.
Native Cultures in Alaska, Vol. 23, No. 2. $19.95.
The Brooks Range, Vol. 23, No. 3. $19.95.
Moose, Caribou and Muskox, Vol. 23, No. 4. $19.95.
Alaska's Southern Panhandle, Vol. 24, No. 1. $19.95.
The Golden Gamble, Vol. 24, No. 2. $19.95.
Commercial Fishing in Alaska, Vol. 24, No. 3. $19.95.
Alaska's Magnificent Eagles, Vol. 24, No. 4. $19.95.
Steve McCutcheon's Alaska, Vol. 25, No. 1. $21.95.
Yukon Territory, Vol. 25, No. 2. $21.95.
Climbing Alaska, Vol. 25, No. 3. $21.95.
Frontier Flight, Vol. 25, No. 4. $21.95. Our 100th Issue!
Restoring Alaska: Legacy of an Oil Spill, Vol. 26, No. 1. $21.95.
World Heritage Wilderness, Vol. 26, No. 2. $21.95.
The Bering Sea, Vol. 26, No. 3. $21.95.

PRICES AND AVAILABILITY SUBJECT TO CHANGE

Membership in The Alaska Geographic Society includes a subscription to *ALASKA GEOGRAPHIC*®, the Society's colorful, award-winning quarterly.

Contact us for current membership rates or to request a free catalog. *ALASKA GEOGRAPHIC*® back issues listed above are also available. **NOTE:** This list was current in late 1999. If more than a year has elapsed since that time, contact us before ordering to check prices and availability of back issues, particularly for books marked "Limited."

When ordering back issues please add $4 for the first book and $2 for each additional book ordered for Priority Mail. Inquire for non-U.S. postage rates. To order, send check or money order (U.S. funds) or VISA/MasterCard information (including expiration date and your phone number) with list of titles desired to:

ALASKA GEOGRAPHIC.

P.O. Box 93370 • Anchorage, AK 99509-3370
Phone: (907) 562-0164 • Fax (907) 562-0479
Toll free (888) 255-6697 • E-mail: info@akgeo.com